MISSING

AN URGENT CALL FOR THE CHURCH TO RESCUE KIDS

MELISSA J. MacDONALD

KUDU

Missing: An Urgent Call for the Church to Rescue Kids
by Melissa J. MacDonald

Copyright © 2014 by Melissa J. MacDonald
Cover design by Martijn van Tilborgh

Published by Kudu Publishing

Print ISBN: 9781938624957
eBook ISBN: 9781938624964

Missing is also available on Amazon Kindle, Barnes & Noble Nook and Apple iBooks.

Missing is a publication of Melissa J. MacDonald Ministries, endorsed by **KIDZMATTER**. For more resources, visit KidzMatter.com and follow us at:

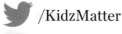 /KidzMatter

 /KidzMatterInc

 /KidzMatter

 /KidzMatter

PRAISE FOR *MISSING*

Jesus pointed to children as the very model of faith that He wanted His disciples (and us!) to follow. He valued them not just as fun little people, but as spiritual beings capable of a deep and abiding faith. Nothing has changed today! And yet, as Melissa points out in this fantastic book, they are the largest unreached people group in the world! It's incredible that, being the largest unreached group *and* the most spiritually receptive, we haven't made them a group of primary focus. This book is a call to action to change that, with a clear message of the importance of the "4-14 Window" and a plan to reach them. Everyone in ministry needs to read this book.

Greg Baird, Senior Director
Program/Leadership Development
Global Church
globalchurch.com

Children's and family ministry is in a peculiar time: we have many tools, incredible resources and noteworthy people inspiring us to develop meaningful ministries. However, the bonds that bring these elements together to formulate a holistic approach for the capital "c" Church are frail. Through her use of personal stories that both clarify and stimulate, Melissa challenges children's leaders to become more deliberate and rethink how we navigate ministry. My passion for children's ministry resonated with this book, and I am confident that this book will make a strategic and intentional difference in your ministry.

Pastor Trevor Lee, Family Life Pastor
Life Community Church, Kirkland, Washington
lifekirkland.org

From pineapple people to fair estimators, the quintessential millennial Melissa J. MacDonald makes us a bit uncomfortable as she tells stories from her life to help us see what the church could be.

Ron Hunter Jr., Executive Director & CEO
Randall House and D6 Conference Director
randallhouse.com

Melissa J. MacDonald has delivered a timely, incisive challenge to children's and family ministry leaders to shepherd the church of today and focus on building momentum to reach children for Jesus Christ. You will not be able to put this book down or walk away from its pages without responding to MacDonald's decisive and inspiring call to action.

Matt Guevara, Executive Director
International Network of Children's Ministry
incm.org

If you are a parent, kids worker or children's pastor, this book is full of information and points of application that will hit home. Each chapter brings you to the same place that Jesus brought His disciples when He denied convention by speaking to the value of children: "Suffer the children to come unto me for such is the kingdom of heaven."

Sam Luce, Utica Campus Pastor
Redeemer Church, Utica, New York
samluce.com

CONTENTS

DEDICATION

DEDICATED TO MY SWEET kiddos scattered all around the world. The hands-on experience of loving you, walking with you and spurring you on to all that God desires for you has shaped me and taught me in ways I hold precious. May you forever remember that you are worth it, you are loved, your choices matter, and God's plans for you are always good, even if they don't always feel good. Both this book and I have been beautifully shaped by you.

ACKNOWLEDGEMENTS

MY THANKS TO KIDZMATTER and Ryan Frank and Martijn van Tilborgh for taking a chance on me and this project. I'm humbled.

Thank you, Lee for spending countless hours editing this book and talking me through the many changes. You are a blessing my friend.

Almost ten years ago I set foot on Whidbey Island and very quickly proclaimed that when I wrote my first book I would write it on the Island. Isn't it just like our God to take my rather naïve statement and bring it to pass? In sight of the Puget Sound with eagles soaring and seals playing this book was written. My deep thanks to the Lynch family and the people at Langley Alliance Church for helping make my crazy dream possible.

I have been "Alliance" my entire life and I have counted it a true joy. To my Alliance family for the many ways you have shaped me, loved me, encouraged me, and released me to soar, thank you. Thank you for seeing in me what I could never have imagined and allowing me to serve you. I am honored.

To the many people such as John Stoeckle and Gordon West and Trevor Lee who asked, "so when are you going to write your book?" Your gentle yet direct words spoken at just the right time were the encouragement I needed to make this happen. Thank you for being bold.

To Steve who always takes time to speak truth and push me forward. Without you this whole project would look very different. Thank you for partnering with me. I promise to stop making fun of your wolf shirts, maybe.

My dear Myriam, thank you for always being excited about this project, never allowing me to take myself too seriously, and for always taking me back to the beauty of the God we serve. You are so dear to me.

In the summer of 2006 I took a chance and welcomed an under qualified and unprepared children's ministry intern to serve under me. While our start wasn't smooth the journey has been oh so sweet. Liz, thank you for being my biggest cheerleader, for having faith when I haven't, for allowing me to verbally process for hours, and for pushing me beyond my limits. Thank you for inspiring me.

To my family. Without your influence, your words, and your daily reflections of Jesus to me I would be much less than what God desires for me. Each one of you is beyond precious and I am so grateful for you. I am honored to be your "Sis," "Sissy," and "Auntie Mo."

To my dedicated prayer team, to my church family at Faith Community Church in Red Oak, Iowa, to my Idaho family and my Florida family, and to my steadfast friends in Minnesota, thank you.

And to my Jesus, for entrusting me with this sacredness; may I be forgettable and may you be ever memorable.

INTRODUCTION

WHEN SOMETHING OR SOMEONE goes missing it's always a call to action. What you do with that call is up to you. This book is a call to action for the church. Kids ages 4 to 14 are now the largest unreached people group in the world and the parents of these kids are Millennials. Over half of Millennials who grew up in the church have since walked away from the church.

Our kids are missing from church, their parents have gone missing, and we as the church are missing the mark. We're on track to lose a generation of kids. This book will make the correlation between what has been and what could be in ministry to kids. I think the crisis of faith many of our young adults are facing today is, in part, directly related to ineffective ministry to kids. The good news about that is that we can learn from our mistakes and move forward with rescue on our hearts and minds.

This is not a "feel-good-about-children's-ministry" book. It's not a "pull yourself up by the bootstraps and muscle on" book. It's not a "grab some coffee and a box of tissues" book. This is an "in your face," "challenge your thinking," "open your eyes," and "rethink everything you thought about ministry" kind of book. It's an urgent call for the church to rescue kids. If we don't, who will?

I invite you to enter in. This is designed to start conversations. Grab a team member, your church staff, another parent, a fellow minister, and dive in together.

CHAPTER 1

I CAN'T HELP BUT START with my very first chapter being a call to the church. I was really gunning for this book to be called *Be the Freaking Church* but after listening to wise council, I decided that might not have been the greatest of marketing plans.

This book is more than a children's ministry book, and I need you as the reader to know that up front. This is a call to the Body of Christ. It's not a comfortable or easy call, but it's a call nonetheless. It is time for the church to start being the church. I'll go on to show you how we've lost a generation and we are on track to lose another one. We need the church.

In the church it's easy to place the responsibility of ministry to kids onto a children's worker or a family ministry pastor and feel good about our intentionality. However, it cannot stop there. We are in crisis mode, and the church can no longer sit by expecting different results by doing the same thing over and over again or, dare I say it, by trying a new curriculum every year expecting that to do the trick.

Think on this: Parents are THE influencers in their kid's lives, whether we like it or not. There are the over-intentional parents, the absent parents, the disengaged parents, the destructive parents, and the good parents. Is the church equipping them, motivating them, resourcing them? If the church isn't, many popular secular speakers, TV personalities, and authors are happy to step in to "help."

Understanding the important role of parents in a child's spiritual walk and engaging the whole family has created the fairly recent rise of "family ministry" in churches. I personally love it! I love what curricula such as D6, Tru, and Orange are doing. I love that churches are beginning to lose the arrogance of, "We'll teach your kids all about Jesus," and are moving toward, "How can we come alongside you as you tell your kids all about Jesus?"

Family ministry is a great movement, but is it enough? My heart has never been able to fully latch onto family ministry alone. It has always been hard for me to contextualize it into my ministry. I've always had the most down-and-out kids drawn to me. The kids with no parents or with parents so disengaged it was highly unlikely I would ever be able to capture and engage them in their child's spiritual walk. I wondered where they fit. I knew they mattered, but how? Where? Why?

We often use Deuteronomy 6:4–9 as our great motivator for spurring parents on to influencing their children's faith. We are quick to put them into the primary role of spiritual influencer. Isn't it easier that way? I do not disagree with that, but I would offer the church a different perspective on the verses. Look again.

"Hear, O Israel: The Lord our God, the Lord is one. Love the Lord your God with all your heart and with all your soul and with all your strength. These commandments that I give you today are to be on your hearts. Impress them on your children. Talk about them when you sit at home and when you walk along the road, when you lie down and when you get up. Tie them as symbols on your hands and bind them on your foreheads. Write them on the door-frames of your houses and on your gates."

The passage does not say "Hear, O parents," it says "Hear, O Israel." It was for the community, not just for the parents. In fact all of Deuteronomy is written to the nation of Israel. Moses is imploring and encouraging the nation to not forget the Lord their God.

The Hebraic community was community driven. They did life together. They had dinner together, they walked along the road together, they saw each other in the evening and in the morning. Our western-thinking minds have a hard time totally understanding that. Where the Hebraic community was family and group oriented, our western minds are "me" centered.

I've heard it argued that while we have difficulty understanding how Mary and Joseph could have lost Jesus at age 12, it wasn't uncommon in that community. In Luke 2:44, it says that they assumed Jesus was in "their company," meaning with the community. They didn't even begin to look for him for over a day. In our western thinking that's hard to comprehend. Let's be honest, we'd be calling DHS on Joseph and Mary today. That was, however, completely normal. The Hebrews did life together.

Maybe instead of calling on Deuteronomy 6 to admonish and motivate parents, we need to be looking at admonishment and motivation for the church. Somewhere along the way we stopped doing life together and started doing life separately. A "family night" is: come to the church, and kids go to the basement, teens go bowling, and parents do a Bible study. Separate corners, separate communities. Kids grow up in the church moving from one separate entity to the next one until suddenly they're supposed to integrate once they graduate from youth group, and we wonder why we're losing them.

Church, we need you. The passing on of faith to the next generation is our responsibility. All of ours. Whether you're 102 or 2, we need you to start being the church. Our kids don't need a great program, great teachers, or a great building, they need us. They need us, as the church, to walk with them, do life with them, pass on faith to them. They need to hear our stories of faith and failure, hope and disgrace. They need us to remind them that even in the deserts of life, our God is the God who saves.

Get the idea out of your head right now that kids are the church of tomorrow; they are not. They are the church of today. You are the church, I am the church, kids are the church. Don't wait around for tomorrow to start doing life in community with them; be the church. I truly believe it will only be within community, operating as the body of Christ that we will ever reach our most lost. Let's be the "freaking" church and change the trajectory we are on.

CHAPTER 2

I n 1990, CHRISTIAN STRATEGIST Luis Bush coined the term "10/40 Window" to refer to the geographical region of the eastern hemisphere, located between 10 and 40 degrees north of the equator, where the largest group of unreached people live. For more than 20 years, missions agencies, denominations, churches, and individual Christians have pulled together to reach the 10/40 Window.

Encouraging indicators show us that the continuing effort is bearing fruit. In 2008, the annual growth rate of Christ followers in the 10/40 Window was almost twice that of outside the 10/40 Window. In 1990, 2.5 percent of the population in the 10/40 Window were Christ followers; in 2005 that number was 4.7 percent. God is at work!

In 2009, Bush urged a new missional focus: the 4/14 Window. Instead of a geographical region, the 4/14 Window refers to a demographic age group. There are 2.3 billion kids in the world, and those aged 4 to 14 are the largest unreached people group today. In the United States, nearly 85 percent of people who make a decision for Christ do so between the ages of 4 and 14. The window of opportunity is huge.

Let's pause for just a moment. We'll be talking about the 4/14 Window throughout this book. The research implications of it are immense, and the attention it's garnering is ministry altering. I want to be very careful, however, that we don't cling to, or worse yet, get hung up on, the age brackets. Yes, all of you analytical thinkers out there, the bracket should be larger than 4–14. Kids before the age of 4 are unreached and kids older than 14 are also unreached. This is simply a point of reference for us. It's a starting point. And after years of very little light being shed on kids, I for one am grateful for the introduction of the 4/14 Window.

When the 10/40 window was revealed, it was a full speed ahead kind of movement throughout missions organizations, denominations, and individuals. The goal was very specific, a geographical region. It was concrete and it was attainable. It gave blessed specific direction. It wasn't easy, but it was clear.

You see, these organizations, denominations, and people knew how to do overseas missions. They had strategies and procedures put into place to reach the unreached. Yes, those strategies and procedures changed based on location, people group, and culture, but the actual act of doing missions was familiar. The 10/40 Window simply provided a new place to focus.

Enter the 4/14 Window. Not intended to take the place of the still very great need to reach those in the 10/40 Window and throughout the world, it once again provides direction. Kids.

Kids. Seems specific enough. Right?

In theory it sounds easy enough. We need to reach kids. Kids are the largest unreached people group in the world today. In actuality, it's much more ambiguous than originally perceived.

Kids. They're little. They're messy. Their noses run. They're a little scary. They're *just* kids.

In my experience, the introduction of the 4/14 Window as a "new" mission field is challenging people in ways the 10/40 Window never did. There is no formula for reaching kids. There is no strategy in place. It's new and it's a little scary. Beyond that is the reality that even if a strategy or formula had already been in place, the simple statistics and facts alone tell us it hasn't been working. So, suddenly we're looking at having to create a whole new way of doing missions, to kids.

(For the purposes of this book, I want to pause and say that when I refer to missions, that encompasses local and global missions. I believe missions is simply being salt and light wherever God has placed you. So missions to kids involves kids in the US and kids around the world.)

I was introduced to the 4/14 Window in early 2010. I read through the booklet that Luis Bush wrote (available as a PDF download from *4to14window.com*) and it was an "aha moment" for me. At the time I was living overseas in Vienna, Austria, working at a Christian international school with kids from over 40 different countries. I am an observer and thinker by nature. I was observing these kids from all around the world and the depth of their lostness broke my heart. In many cases we were starting from scratch to even begin to establish any kind of biblical worldview. It was challenging, but it wasn't all that different from ministry to kids in the US. Gone were the days where kids at least had a base knowledge of the Bible and of God.

I was six years old when I first felt God calling me to be a missionary. I was young, but I was determined. I knew that's what God wanted me to do and, honestly, I was that type of kid, youth, young adult, who very rarely doubted what I knew God said to me. I moved through life intent on my goal. I was fulfilling my required home service before going overseas when God began to speak to my heart and whisper a different kind of dream.

I was a children's pastor and I absolutely loved my job. I approached it with an almost reverent solemnity. I was watching God begin to touch and change kids' lives and in turn touch and change families, and my mind began turning. I began to observe that if the kids were content, the parents would choose to attend that church. In most cases if the kids were happy, momma and daddy were happy. After over 15 years with an undying passion for the mission field, my heart and my mind often strategized in relation to overseas ministry. I began to dream about doing children's ministry overseas in a larger capacity than just one field/city/church. What might that look like?

I took this idea to my leaders and while it wasn't totally new to them, things weren't exactly put into place for this to be easily done. The bottom line was, very little was being done to reach kids overseas. I didn't like it and I wanted it to be different.

Fast forward to when I read the 4/14 Window booklet and I knew the research was onto something. I knew that booklet had the power to shake organizations and denominations to the core. It wasn't a clearly defined goal, it wasn't cut and dried, and it certainly wasn't going to be easy. Regardless of all of that, it couldn't be ignored.

I've sat down with leaders, pastors, elders, parents, etc., and once they're exposed to the 4/14 Window, they wanted to know what to do about it. That's the beauty of being able to educate people: It usually leads to some sort of action.

So what do we do about the 4/14 Window? It starts with being informed and being aware. The church must be aware of what's going on around us. This is the reality. Like it or not, kids are the largest unreached people group in the world and they're the most receptive to the Gospel. So whether you're afraid of them, find them obnoxious, or would rather they are seen and not heard, you cannot ignore this mission field. And for those of you who love kids, love teaching them about Jesus, and love reaching them, get ready. That millennial crisis I mentioned in the intro? It's about to rock your world and the way you pass on faith to kids.

CHAPTER 3

THE GENERATION BORN BETWEEN 1980 and 2000 is considered Millennials. Those dates can shift a bit depending on what research you're reading. In some studies I'm a Millennial and in others I've just missed the mark.

As a Millennial, I'm the last person to try to box in an entire generation (Millennials really hate being told how and where they're supposed to fit. Don't fence us in.) I don't want to overgeneralize a generation, but for the purposes of this book, I will be referring to young adults—who are considered a part of the Millennial generation.

Like generations who have gone before, the Millennial generation has unique distinctions. According to the Pew Research Center, Millennials are confident, self-expressive, liberal, upbeat, and open to change. They're less religious than older adults and are "on track to become the most educated generation in American history."[1]

---

1. *http://pewsocialtrends.org/files/2010/10/millennials-confident-connected-open-to-change.pdf*

Millennials are extremely connected. Technology, social media, and digital advancements define who they are. Their cell phones or tablets seem to be one of their body parts. They're social, although that socialness may not refer to actually spending time with another person outside of technology.

Parents and leaders have been concerned about the faith development of Millennials for quite some time. Their concern has not been without merit. Barna research shows us that 59 percent of young people who grew up in a Christian church will end up walking away from either their faith or church as an institution at some point in their adult life. Most likely, that walking away will happen during their first decade as an adult. The number of Millennials who are unchurched has increased in the last decade from 44 to 52 percent. The cultural trend is moving away from church going.[2]

There is no single reason why Millennials have chosen to walk away from the church. Instead Barna has provided a list of six reasons.

#1. Churches seem overprotective. *Millennials desire for their faith to connect with their world.*

#2. Teens' and twentysomethings' experience of Christianity is shallow. *Something was lacking in their church experience. It was boring and irrelevant.*

#3. Churches come across as antagonistic to science. *There is tension between faith and science that the church does not address or seem to even allow.*

---

2. *https://www.barna.org/barna-update/millennials/635-5-reasons-millennials-stay-connected-to-church#. UlR6amTF3Cc*

#4. Young Christians' church experiences related to sexuality are often simplistic, judgmental. *There is tension between living meaningful lives in terms of sexuality and sex and the wholesomeness and abstinence the church preaches.*

#5. Millennials wrestle with the exclusive nature of Christianity. *Culture values open-mindedness and tolerance; the church does not.*

#6. The church feels unfriendly to those who doubt. *It's not a safe place to ask questions and wrestle with doubts.*

We know a percentage of Millennials are leaving the church. There is also a percentage who are staying behind and have a deep walk with the Lord. Barna also includes five ways church communities can build deeper relationships with Millennials and help them stay connected to the church. (More details on each of these is available at www.barna.org.)

#1. Make room for meaningful relationships. *Relational positive church experiences.*

#2. Teach cultural discernment. *Help them develop discernment skills.*

#3. Make reverse mentoring a priority. *Help them find their place in serving and give them opportunities to serve, now.*

#4. Embrace the potency of vocational discipleship. *Teach theology of vocation and/or calling.*

#5 Facilitate connections with Jesus. *Facilitate a deeper sense of intimacy with God.*

I realize I just gave you a bunch of research and lists. I firmly believe we must be students of our work. Our work is raising kids; Millennials are the grown-up kids we've been raising.

The more we know about them, the better we know how to adjust for and equip the next generation. Our job as ministers to children is to intentionally strive to reach them in the most effective ways possible.

I mentioned earlier I'm either a Millennial, or right on the cusp of one, depending on the research parameters. I find myself identifying more with the Millennial Generation than I do with Generation X. I'm connected, I'm educated, I'm diverse, I'm inclusive, I push the limits, I purposely look for different, for other. In many ways both my generational identity and my personality give me a proclivity to look out of the box when it comes to kids and how we reach them. I highly respect those who have gone before and who were the pioneers of their time. I respect them, while understanding that in their time what they were doing was effective. I respect them, while gently pointing out research such as the above and asking us to pioneer and forge ahead once more.

I don't like to dwell on mistakes and the past, but I do want to be a student of those past mistakes in order to not make them again. I also want to celebrate the victories and learn from those. I want to be a learner and a thinker. We must not settle for the status quo and "what we've always done" when it comes to children's ministry. We have to be striving for more. We have to be willing to look backwards with the intention of moving forward.

CHAPTER 4

THE 4/14 WINDOW IS a frame of reference, and it's a reality. Luis Bush is a gifted and trusted researcher. It can't be denied. Now our job is to take this information and do something with it. The ball is in our court.

I was a children's pastor for a total of six years in both Florida and then in Idaho. Then I went overseas to serve as Elementary Chaplain and Counselor at the International Christian School of Vienna. I'm a pastor's kid. I grew up in the type of pastor's family where we did ministry together. We, as a unit, were pastors. I started working with kids when I was seven. I was one of the supremely obnoxious kids who was so responsible and put together (in every area except my dress; thanks mom) that it made complete sense to have me serving in our ministry to young moms group. I was lead teaching children's church by the time I was 12 and bossing around my "helper" (70-year-old Elvera) by the time I was 14. All that to say, I know ministry and I know kids.

I was never one of those ministers who focused solely on my own specific ministry. I love the church in general and I love people in general. So while I was working with kids (12 and under), I was also mentoring teenagers, hanging with the over fifty club, involved in a small group, and I was even invited to the men's group every now and then. I've always been holistic in my approach to ministry.

So I felt like my reading should be holistic as well. Yes, I read children's ministry books, but I also read other books about ministry and leadership. I became a student of all ages, especially the ages my kids would be going into immediately following children's ministry. I devoured books about teens and young adults and their challenges and struggles. I felt like if I could understand what they were going through, I could better prepare my kids for those ages.

Through that reading I began to consider the whole "millennial crisis." Kids were disappearing from the church once they graduated from high school. Perhaps it was just me, but I was not okay with kids I had poured my heart and soul into walking away from the Jesus I had pointed them to. Books like *Sticky Faith, You Lost Me, Already Gone,* and *Almost Christian* became my textbooks. It seemed to me that if I could find out why they were walking away, perhaps I could prevent it for the next generation. Maybe, just maybe, I could change the statistics.

In Barna's book *Transforming Children into Spiritual Champions*, he stresses the fact that before the age of 13, kids are forming what they believe. After age 13, they start defending what they believe.

We've all seen it happen, right? Those of us in kids' ministry can usually watch it happen in fifth or sixth grade. These sweet little cherubs we are ministering to suddenly begin to change before our eyes. They no longer agree with everything we say. They no longer sit before us crisscross applesauce with notebooks and eager expressions that say, "teach us, oh wise one." Things begin to change.

God created the human brain to question, to "rebel." It's simply physiology. We can fight it, whine about it, and moan about how our cherubs have become minions overnight, or we can embrace it. It's the very presence of God at work in them. By nature they are going to start defending what they now believe.

I will fully admit to the fact that I am much more a proactive person than a reactive person. That is one of the reasons why I am so passionate about working with kids. I absolutely love ministry to teens and I mentor quite a few girls, but as I am mentoring them, I am already fighting against the foundation they are defending. So many of their core issues relate back to what they learned in their formative years.

As a children's ministry innovator, I have laughingly called myself Smokey the Bear. Smokey the Bear is the mascot of the United States Forest Service. He educates the public about fire prevention and the dangers of forest fires. He's famous for his slogan, "only YOU can prevent forest fires." Prevention is the key to preventing forest fires. I believe that in ministry, the key to preventing crises is also prevention. I work with kids because I get to be in the business of prevention instead of the business of fighting fires. Someone described it to me as, "I'd rather build a fence at the top of the mountain than do triage at the bottom."

As people who work with kids, we get the incredible opportunity to partner with parents to create a foundation of faith in our kids' little hearts that will affect them for the rest of their lives. I still get goose bumps whenever I think about it. What an amazing opportunity. It's not just about a good story, or a verse memorized—it's about molding the very core of who these kids become, what they know about Jesus, and how they live their lives. It's awesome, in every sense of that word.

I rolled all of these thoughts, statistics, and books into one and came to the conclusion that I stated in the introduction. *I think the crisis of faith many of our young adults are facing today is, in part, directly related to ineffective ministry to kids.* Now is the time for action.

I'm not content with our millennial crisis. I'm not content with the 4/14 Window, and therefore I'm not content with doing ministry the way it's always been done when it's clear the way it's been done isn't working. Yes, I know, we all have our token stories of God's grace evident in the lives of the people we minister to. We hold onto those tokens and are so grateful for them. But perhaps, we're holding on so tightly, we can't see beyond them. We can't see beyond our few token kids, teens, adults to see that although they are precious, they are an exception to the rule, not the rule. Perhaps we need to allow ourselves to become a little uncomfortable with the ones we've lost instead of feeling comfortable with the ones we've gained.

The simple fact of the matter is we've lost a generation (millennials) and we are losing another (4/14 Window). To say we're in a crisis is putting it mildly. It's time for the church to wake up. It's time for missions organizations and denominations and church leaders to wake up. The time is now and the place it starts is with kids. Don't hear me saying to quit reaching the older generations, but do understand that the answer to where we're heading starts with the generation of today, our very littlest ones.

KIDS

If we're serious about reaching the 4/14 Window for Jesus, passing on faith, and preventing another millennial crisis, we must first and foremost start with kids. Humans are at their most teachable and moldable stage as children. That foundational age is the place to start.

Somewhere along the way we started seeing kids as some sort of a "less than" entity. They're little, their brains aren't fully developed, they're hard to control, and after all, they're just kids.

When we use comments like that, we are either consciously or unconsciously limiting a child's ability to learn, perceive, grow, and be. We're putting them in a box of "not enough" and "unable."

Is that fair?

Think about it for a minute. What's the most important decision you'll ever make in your life?

No it's not buying your car, marrying your spouse, or even deciding to go into ministry. The most important decision you'll ever make in your life is to start a relationship with Jesus. That decision trumps them all. It's your cornerstone, the rock you have built your life and ministry upon, and it decides your destiny for eternity. Big deal.

Remember, 85 percent of people who make a decision to follow Jesus do so between the ages of 4 and 14.

Do you see that percentage? Do you see that age bracket? That means that the most important decision you've ever made in your life was most likely made when you were a kid.

A kid.

God doesn't base a child's ability to love and serve Him on age. Why should we?

I made the biggest, most impactful, most life-altering decision of my life at the age of five. Five! I knew nothing about theology, the Trinity, or the beauty of an atoning sacrifice. I simply wanted to know Jesus and be a part of His family. That was enough. That started a lifelong journey to know more of Him. A journey that started when I was a runny-nosed five year old trying to boss around the entire church.

At five, I wanted more.

It seems pretty clear to me that God doesn't underestimate kids, so why should we? Why would we put limitations on the very ones about whom Jesus said "let them come to me, don't hinder them"?

Who better to understand the heart of the Father but a little one? Unlike adults, they don't have fences and walls from past hurts and hang-ups that they have to try to break down or scale in order to understand Jesus' love for them. They're self-centered in the most beautiful of ways. In a way that doesn't question that the God of the entire universe would want to have a relationship with them. That the very one who carved the seas and sees all, has time and takes delight in listening to their simple prayers.

Children love without condition. They accept and they believe. It's precious. It's sacred. It's inspiring.

Children have the capacity for more. Perhaps it is we adults who limit them. Perhaps they're not limited by their size, their age, or their ability, but by us.

In the next few chapters we're going to talk about passing on faith and give you practical examples for what kids need in order to change the course we're on. I'm not going to give you a curriculum, a program, or even a to-do list. I'm simply going to give you ideas to consider as you rethink how you do ministry to kids and how you pass on faith.

CHAPTER 5

W E NEED CRITICAL THINKERS. We need to be passing on faith and raising up kids who know how to think. We need to be raising up kids who know why it's important to think. We need to be raising up kids who think critically about the world around them. Society encourages kids at school to think critically, but the church does not do this effectively, therefore a distinct gap is created between a child's two worlds church and school/social life. As the church we need to encourage and foster critical thinking.

I was a lazy kid. I'll admit it with full disclosure here. I had a bit of a pie-in-the-sky attitude and took to heart whatever I heard as long as it was from a somewhat trustworthy source. I wasn't taught to think about things. I could blame my parents who answered my "Why?" questions with the age-old, "Because I said so." Yes, I suppose in part, my laziness was their fault. I'm the type of learner who learns by asking questions. As a kid I'm sure I seemed completely obnoxious and even disrespectful at times. It was easier to say, "Because I said so," than it was to explain things to me.

However, it cannot all be blamed on my parents. I was also just plain lazy. I accepted what was told to me and never gave it much thought. I had significant respect for those in authority over me so what they said impacted me and mattered. It was all well and good until I went to college.

I entered college as a rather naïve former homeschooler. I went to a Christian school for elementary school and then was homeschooled until I graduated. I was not unsocialized by any means. I was highly involved at church and had been working at the local grocery store for a number of years. I knew how to be with people. I also knew what I believed and could not be swayed.

I went to Crown College in Minnesota, a small Christian Bible college, for my undergrad. I went in knowing what I believed. Where I was challenged was in the "why" part of my beliefs. I couldn't back any of my beliefs up. I knew abortion was wrong, but I couldn't give you solid reasoning for why. I knew I needed to be involved in a local church, but I didn't know why. I was a lazy thinker.

I remember taking a critical thinking class where we had to evaluate essays, and I so wanted to do it and do it well. It was like trying to walk through mud to get my brain to think. It was an incredible struggle to get my brain to engage and critically think. Academics had always come easy to me, but this class homework took me hours to do with many tears, questions, and frustration.

I left that class with one of the lowest grades in my college career, but with the most amount of pride. The struggle had been worth it and in the process, I went from lazy to engaged. Like using a muscle, I had to intentionally force myself to think critically about things and search for the "why."

When I became a children's pastor, one of my greatest desires was to train and raise up kids who could think critically. I had been so incredibly shocked by my college discovery that I knew I wanted to prepare kids to think. Well before Barna's research told me of the need for it, I began training kids to think.

I use the word "training" loosely because I didn't necessarily have a plan or a strategy beyond teaching kids to think. What it really boiled down to was pretty simple: questions. I began asking kids questions.

A controversial movie came out during one of my years as a children's pastor. It was one of those movies everyone was talking about. Parents were buzzing about it, kids were buzzing about it, and the Christian community was buzzing about it. In fact, I got an e-mail from a respected national Christian group asking children's pastors and youth pastors to tell their students to not attend the movie. I read the e-mail and immediately didn't like it. It was like a bell went off in my head for the very first time, and I knew I wasn't going to do that. I knew from my own experience that a simple "no" did nothing more than frustrate. I wanted my kids to think about it instead.

That week I went into our after-school preteen group with the sole intention of talking with kids about the movie. Nothing more, nothing less. I had no idea how it was going to turn out or if you could even do something like that with fourth, fifth, and sixth graders, but I was determined to try.

I sat them all down and brought up the movie and asked them what they thought. You could hear a pin drop as their eyes shuffled frantically around the room avoiding me and looking at their friends. Poor little things had never had to think for themselves in our group before, and they had no idea what to do. I had mercy on them and asked the same question a different way. I did it in a relaxed way looking nonchalant as I leaned back in my chair. They had no idea that beads of sweat were forming on my back as I was desperately trying to figure out what we were going to do once this completely failed.

Finally one of my little guys said, "I think it's a bad movie."

I let out a huge sigh of relief. It wasn't much, but it was enough. I followed up his statement with another exploratory question and then another and before I knew it we were having a rousing conversation. What I loved most of all was that our conversation had started with the movie, but it quickly moved into opening our Bibles to see what the Word had to say about certain things, talking about respecting our parent's authority, and discussing making wise decisions for ourselves.

I shared openly about how I couldn't watch scary movies because even as an adult, they scared me in a non-funny way. I explained that I had made the decision for myself to not watch scary movies, so that I would not be afraid, and so that I could sleep at night. I had learned what I could and could not handle. As soon as I shared that, one of my other adult leaders opened up with boundaries he had in place because he'd learned what he could and could not handle. Then the kids opened up and began sharing, and our little room became a safe place.

By the end of the afternoon, each kid knew whether or not they were going to see that movie and why. They were well informed about what was in it, what was wrong with it, what wasn't okay in it, and they had made their decisions. (Note: I made it very clear that no matter their decision, mom and dad's decision still always trumps their own.) They left empowered and with knowledge that went far beyond just that particular movie.

That started the "revolution of questions" in my work with kids. It's something that has yet to stop.

ASK QUESTIONS

The more questions I ask and am asked, I realize that the issue is no longer training kids to think—it's giving them permission to think. We are pretty quick to shut down their questions for a variety of reasons. It's not in our lesson plans, they have so many questions, and some of us, let's just be honest, don't know how to answer their questions.

None of us were created to be lazy thinkers. God created us to ask, explore, inquire, discover, and push. Kids by nature are questioners. "Why?" and "How come?" are constantly pouring out of their mouths. We can pass them off as obnoxious or we can run with it and understand that's part of their learning process. We need to foster their critical thinking.

ALLOW THEM TO ASK QUESTIONS

I was recently speaking to a camp of fifth and sixth graders. I gave them slips of paper and asked them to write down some of the big questions they had in their hearts and their minds about

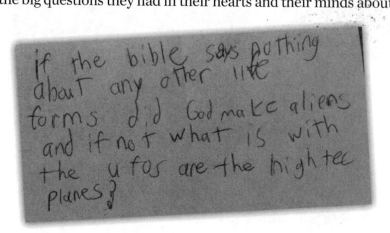

If God didn't create us, would he still love us?

How does God control our lives and why?

How long did God live alone without anyone with him?

Why does God wait for the right moment to make something good come out of the bad?

How do you fully die to yourself?

Why did god creat us is we were just to die.

if I feel insecure about myself what can I say to god that will help me?

God or life. I expected to get a couple back. What I did not expect was how many questions would be jammed onto those little slips of papers and just how deep those questions would go.

I was blown away by the depth and breadth of their questions.

"Why did God create us if we were just to die?"

"What do I do when my friend says she's not my friend anymore?"

"What does it mean to receive grace?"

"How do I fully die to myself?"

"Why did God create us?"

"Why do I still do bad things when I don't want to?"

"What's up with aliens?"

I went to the first chapel after getting the initial onslaught of questions (they never stopped coming throughout the week) and asked how many of them lie in bed at night with big questions in their heads. There was literally a collective gasp and a "ME!" as hands shot up everywhere. A bunch of them yelled, "All the time!"

BE SILENT

The next day kids were asking questions when one little girl shot her hand in the air. I called on her and her question was simple, "What's the meaning of life?"

Good grief! A hundred thoughts ran through my head, the most prominent one being, "Why did I call on her?" Her questions silenced the kids like nothing else had that week. Suddenly I had 200 pairs of eyes staring at me. I did what any self-respecting, panicking speaker would do; I told them we would answer that tomorrow, and I went on with my regular speaking schedule.

That night and the next morning I agonized over how to answer that question. I went for a long walk, I prayed, I researched, I called my pastor dad, and I groaned. By the end of all my whining and preparation, I was ready. *I always try to be as prepared as possible and as interruptible as possible.* Desiring to leave room for the Holy Spirit to work. I had a three-point outline and was ready to face the little eyes.

I clearly remember stepping up to speak to them. I asked them, "Who remembers the question from yesterday?" praying that by some miracle they would have all come down with temporary amnesia. No such luck. All of them chorused, "What's the meaning of life?"

I opened my mouth to begin when God clearly interrupted me and said, "You need to be silent."

In a split second I had a heated, mostly one-sided, silent argument with God. "What!? But I'm ready now. Lord, that's not nice. You gave me a voice so I'm using it! What am I supposed to say? Are you SURE?"

"You need to be silent."

I argued, but it didn't 't take me too long to come under His authority. I calmly shut the notebook on my three-point outline and looked at the kids.

"What makes me important?" I quietly asked them, "What makes me matter?"

"You can speak and tell us about Jesus! "

"What if I couldn't speak anymore? What if my voice was gone forever? What would make me important?"

"You could write things. You could tell people stories by writing."

"What if my hands quit working? Would I still matter? Would I still be important?"

The dialogue continued. I did very little but to guide it a tiny bit. Toward the end of our conversation, I was a vegetable. I had no working functions; I wasn't even breathing on my own. I was confined to a bed and couldn't even blink.

"Do I still matter?"

All the kids yelled out, "Yes!"

"Why?"

The silence that followed that question shook me to my core. I was frantically asking God if I could answer it while He was steadily telling me to be silent. I then began praying for something, anything to come from that group. They began discussing with one another, ignoring me standing there completely vulnerable, desperately wanting to tell them the answer. Finally one fourth grade boy in the back got the courage to raise his hand.

I called on him and you could tell he was thinking and processing as he answered, "I think you matter because you were created by God and you matter because He loves you. You matter because you matter to Him?"

My knees sagged and tears filled my eyes. "Stand up and say it louder."

He repeated it more confidently this time and a couple of kids around him were nodding.

With a lump in my throat I emphatically said, "That is the meaning of life. We're here for Him. We matter because we matter to Him."

The hushed silence that followed can only be described as a holy moment. You could watch them *get it*. It was by far the most defining moment of that camp and that summer for me. Three days later as parents were picking their kids up, they were running out saying, "I know the meaning of life!"

You don't have to have all the answers. You don't have to know it all. You just have to be willing to be used.

Somewhere in the midst of kids thinking collectively and answering the big questions, pieces of their foundations begin to settle and lock into place. It's like watching a child tie a shoe for the first time. You can watch as these kids begin to step out in pride and realize they do know the answers, or are at least willing to try. Critical thinking takes place when we ask questions, let them ask questions, and stay silent. That passes on faith.

CHAPTER 6

WE NEED TO EMPOWER kids. They need to believe they can change the world.

This is always a challenging part for me to talk about because it can be easily misconstrued. I do not believe we need to stand in a circle with children and sing "We Are the World," and I do not believe we should be telling kids they can be anything they want to be. There is a clear line between honesty and a condescending pat on the back.

I talked earlier about how kids are self-centered in a beautiful way. It's true, they are. I love the boy who believes he's going to be a football player/firefighter/chef when he grows up and the girl who believes she'll be a dancer/veterinarian/doctor when she grows up. It's adorable and their dreams speak to just how big they dream. I love it.

The sad thing about our culture today is that those fanciful dreams are fewer and further apart. Real life is hitting kids at such a young age. Kids' home lives are a mess. Fifty percent of all the children born to married parents today will experience the divorce of their parents before they are 18 years old (Fagan, Fitzgerald, Rector, *The Effects of Divorce on America*).

MISSING

Bullying is at an all-time high at school. It is estimated that every day 160,000 children miss school due to fear of attack or intimidation by other students (National Education Association). These kids who are growing up in this mess only know to emulate what they see. It's a vicious cycle.

The tendency in this case would be to make life and the world seem as easy and as friendly as possible to kids. Let them escape in any way they need to in order to survive. Is that wise? Is it responsible? Is it kind?

Perhaps more than any other generation, this one is crying out for authenticity. They're desperate for it. We have all watched the popular talent shows on television where people get up and audition by singing. They've been told by everyone who loves them that they're amazing, their voices are angelic, their moves are fantastic, and there is no way they won't win the next big title. They take the stage and all of America waits for them to start singing. They open their mouth and what comes out more closely resembles an animal in pain than it does singing. The crowd boos, the judges laugh, and you grab for the mute button. Meanwhile the person auditioning cannot understand why people didn't like their "singing." They go off stage and their whole family grabs them and hugs them and tells them how wrong the judges were.

That's our culture today. We care more about making people feel good about themselves than we do about honesty. Kids are being raised with this idea that they're right and everyone else around them is wrong. There is little regard for honesty. Kids don't need fluff; they need, and want, real, honest feedback. Life comes at them fast, and it's only going to get faster. We need to be preparing kids for the world, and their part in the world instead of allowing them to think they ARE the world.

I'll never forget going to the doctor for my kindergarten check-up. I was so excited to start kindergarten that I could barely sit still in the doctor's office. I thought I had heard something about shots, but I was too antsy to really think about it. The nurse put me on the examining table and had me look at a picture that had little sheep in it. I remember her talking about the dumb sheep all the while swabbing my arm. I was no dummy as a kid, and I knew the woman was trying to distract me from something. I went along with it, however and looked at the fluffy little sheep. I was counting them when she jabbed the needle into my arm and pushed down the plunger. As any self-respecting five year old would do, I screamed bloody murder. I don't actually remember it hurting, but I do remember being extremely mad. I was mad they had tried to distract me, I was mad I didn't know what was coming, and I was mad that I wasn't prepared.

Even as an adult, I can still recall how angry I was. It didn't feel fair that nobody warned me and told me what was coming.

That's what's happening to kids in our world today. We're not preparing them for what's coming. We're so busy trying to distract them with the sheep and make them feel good that they're entirely unprepared for reality.

How can kids change the world if they're not even aware of the world?

Please note, I am not suggesting you send kids out for a crash course in real life. We absolutely must be responsible with their little hearts and minds. Part of that responsibility is training them for real life in age level appropriate ways.

Kids need to be empowered, and they need to truly believe they can change the world. They need truth in a world rife with narcissism. Brene Brown says in her book *Daring Greatly*:

I can see exactly how and why more people are wrestling with how to believe they are enough. I see the cultural messaging everywhere that says that an ordinary life is a meaningless life. And I see how kids that grow up on a steady diet of reality television, celebrity culture, and unsupervised social media can absorb this messaging and develop a completely skewed sense of the word. *I am only as good as the number of "likes" I get on Facebook or Instagram.*

I believe kids can change the world. I believe it because I've seen it. The whole foundational piece cannot be ignored here. If we can help build into their foundation truth and love and the essence of Jesus, and they understand that they are a part of something bigger than themselves, that changes the world.

Here's an example for you. One of the biggest things I struggled to understand as an adult was that hurt people hurt people. Seems simple enough, right? In reality, it's hard and messy and extremely hurtful. As an adult I didn't get it. If someone hurt me once it was shame on them, twice it was shame on me, and I washed my hands of them.

It wasn't until I really dove into my master's work in counseling that I began to see the damaging effects of hurt and unforgiveness and a hard childhood. God broke my heart for people and I finally understood that hurt people hurt people. It completely changed the way I approached people. Instead of anger I felt compassion, and instead of lashing out I would more often turn to prayer. I was amazed at the power a kind word and prayer could have on hurt people.

I truly believed that if I could help kids grasp the concept of hurt people hurt people, that would begin to change the world. Call me crazy, but I started to teach that. It all started with a pineapple.

Not too many years ago I was following God's call on my life and I was doing a lot of waiting. During that time of my life I was doing anything and everything to make my children's ministry consulting and training a reality. To say money was tight would be a gross understatement. I was working multiple part-time jobs, grocery "shopping" in my parent's pantry, and clinging faithfully to God's promises for me.

One of those jobs was in a grocery store. I started working at our local grocery store in my home town of Red Oak, Iowa, when I was 15. I worked there steadily even on breaks from college. When I moved back home as an adult with no money and only a dream, the grocery store graciously agreed to hire me back on. So back to work I went. Given the economy of our town during that time, I can only say I was extremely grateful for the job.

Unbeknownst to me, I had a knack for fruit cutting, and I was offered a 25 cents per hour raise and was promoted to "official fruit cutter." There I was chopping away at pineapples praying about what God would lay on my heart to speak to the kids at a camp I was slated to be at a couple of months later and I had an epiphany. People are a lot like pineapples.

I met Kendra when she was eight. She started attending my after-school youth group for fourth, fifth, and sixth graders. She was scrappy, unruly, and mean. Seriously, she was a mean eight year old. She had an attitude a mile long and a penchant for disrespect. Like a pineapple, she was prickly. Every time I tried to get close to her, she'd poke me and I'd withdraw, not willing to get pricked again. I put her in other volunteers' small groups and was civil to her, but I did not like her. God clearly spoke to my heart that I needed to be praying to develop a love for her. With great reluctance this was my prayer, "God I don't like Kendra, help me love her ... if you can. Give me your eyes for her."

MISSING

Short and sweet, I'm not proud of that prayer, but it was all my poked heart and pride could handle. I prayed it as often as I remembered and always after prickly Kendra poked me.

One Saturday I drove a van load of kids home from a weekend retreat. We pulled into the church singing loudly and laughing about weekend "you had to be there" jokes. All the parents were lined up in the parking lot waiting for their kids. The van unloaded in a spill of preteen smell and cuteness. When there were no parents left, I was gathering up the lost and found items, and then I saw Kendra. She was standing by the van looking forlorn.

It had been a long weekend dealing with her and all the other kids. I was tired and I wanted her gone. I literally said, "Kendra, why are you still here? Go home!"

"I don't know where my parents are Miss Mel."

I tossed her my cell phone and told her to get them called and get them here. I went back to my gathering of lost items wondering how kids managed to lose underwear every year.

Kendra came up to me holding my phone a moment later.

"Who's coming to get you Kendra?"

She looked at the ground and stiffly said, "My dad says it's my mom's weekend and my mom says it's my dad's weekend. Nobody wants me." Her lip was quivering at this point, and my heart broke wide open as a tear slipped down her cheek.

I gathered her awkwardly into my arms, neither one of us was used to hugging the other. I held her as she sobbed. Tears coursed down my own cheeks. For the first time, I saw her, I really saw Kendra. With the eyes of Jesus, I saw all of the hurt she had inside, and I understood why she was so prickly.

Pineapples have little circles on their outside skin. Those circles hold in moisture so if the rains aren't regular pineapples have life-giving water stored up. Those circles put out little spikes to protect the skin and moisture. Pineapples are uniquely created by God to protect themselves and to keep enemies out. If you're willing to push through all of the defenses of a pineapple, you'll find pure deliciousness and sweetness inside. Most people prefer to buy it precut to avoid cuts, scrapes, and the hassle.

Kendra was a pineapple. She had received so very little love throughout her life, she had stored up what she could and put out spikes so she wouldn't get hurt again. That girl was one bundle of spikes that were hiding a world of hurt. Hurt people hurt people. She didn't need me to lash out at her and respond in anger to her pokes; she needed me to love her unconditionally.

That day in the parking lot changed everything for me. My heart broke open, and it's yet to be "fixed." I got it, I saw, and I was changed. Kendra didn't change. In fact in some ways she got worse, but I saw her completely differently and my love for her was unchanging and constant. I prayed for her out of love and compassion, and slowly but surely God began a work. The prickles started to go away, healing began, and Kendra began to change. She started a relationship with Jesus, and it's made all the difference in her. Her circumstances are still unsure, but she's solid.

Kendra and I remain close to this day. She's one of my dearest girls. While writing this book, I was able to visit her. She told me about how God is using her in the lives of other youth. She's on fire for Jesus, and nothing is stopping her. She calls me regularly to cry, pray, share, etc. We sing to each other on our birthdays, Snapchat ugly pictures of ourselves, and sit with our hands intertwined at Starbucks with tears ruining our makeup as she tells me all about what Jesus is doing in and through her.

She was a pineapple who needed a little love. Hurt people hurt people, and they need us to love them, pray for them, and show compassion to them. That changes the world around us.

Can you imagine a generation of kids who understand that "hurt people hurt people" and "Pineapple People" need our love and prayers? Can you imagine how that might change the world? It's crazy cool to think about it. It's even more amazing to see it happening. I share about Pineapple People everywhere I am asked to speak to kids. Pineapple People has gone around the world. It's been used in international schools, mission fields, college campuses, camps, churches, etc.

After I spoke about it at one camp, a little third grade girl came up to me. You could tell she was thinking and remembering as she was talking to me. "Miss Mel, I live with my grandpa. I can't live with my mom."

"Okay."

"I remember I got taken away because my mom used to pick me up by the hair and throw me down the stairs. I used to have to wait until my mom was asleep so I could sneak downstairs and get food for my baby brother."

I kept listening while my heart was breaking wide open.

"Know what Miss Mel?"

"What's that sweetie?"

"My mom's mom hurt her a lot when she was a little girl. I think my mom hurts me because she was hurt by her mom. I think she might be my pineapple person. I think God might be telling me I need to pray for her and forgive her. Do you think she could be my pineapple person?"

"I absolutely do."

We prayed together and I shut the door to have a good long cry.

It's a hard story, but do you see the beauty of that? A third grader grasping the concept of hurt people hurting people and understanding what she can do. She's praying faithfully for her mom and praying that she'll be able to forgive her. That's beautiful. (Note: there's a fine line between loving and praying for a Pineapple Person and purposely putting yourself in harm's way. It's important to talk kids through the difference.)

Pineapple People is by far the number one thing I hear back from kids about. It affects adults as well. While writing this I received a text from a 21 year old who thanked me for Pineapple People and how it's challenging him in his life. I get e-mails and texts and even phone calls about people praying for their Pineapple People and God working in their lives. Does that change the world? You better believe it does.

What if we passed on faith and raised up a generation that understood that the very people who hurt us the most are the ones who need our love and prayer the most? It would change the face of almost every single life situation. Shouldn't we be building that into the foundation of kids so that it is simply a part of who they are? That changes the world. That equips kids for reality and to be world changers.

Pineapple People is just one of 100 ways you can empower kids to change the world. The power of intentionality cannot be ignored here. Take a minute to jot down some ideas you have for how to pass on faith and empower kids to be world changers.

CHAPTER 7

WE NEED TO PASS on faith and raise up kids who understand they have the power to make wise choices.

Our freedom to choose is what defines us as humans and as individuals. When God created us He made us fully human and gave us free will. Instead of creating robots, God gave us the ability to choose. This has resulted in both catastrophic events and wonderful events. Whatever the outcome, God allows us to choose.

Whether kids are aware of it or not, they make choices every day. How will they treat their friends? What words will they use when they speak to their parents? Will they tell the truth about the broken bike or not?

As much as we'd prefer to have tiny robots who do everything we say, children have free will and will make their own choices. In fact, it's very hard to force a kid to do anything he or she doesn't want to do. They're already making choices. Why not train them to make wise choices instead of choosing for them?

Every time I'm asked to talk to kids, I talk about choices. It's my go-to subject, not because it's easy, it's actually quite challenging, but because I believe it is so important. As kids we're told what to do, when to do it, how to do it, and just do it! We're young and we need that authority and protection in our lives. The responsibility of the adult is to find the fine line between telling and explaining, forcing and equipping.

Remember that the biggest decision you will ever make in your life will most likely be made when you are a child. A child gets to choose to start a relationship with Jesus. It's their choice. Our job is to let them know they get to make that choice.

It's easy to coerce kids. Kids are gullible, easily scared, and easily swayed. When I speak to kids, I could easily get an entire camp of second and third graders to ask Jesus into their hearts. All I would need to do is talk about hell and how horrible it is and describe what life for eternity without Jesus would be like. Then I would tell a story, play some soft music, and have kids repeat after me. Kids look around at other kids who are crying or have their hands up and everyone joins in. I could then walk away feeling like we just had a major revival happen, when in fact I may have done more manipulation than explanation and invitation.

Instead, whenever I talk to kids about starting a relationship with Jesus, I always tell them it's their choice. I lay the decision out with as much honesty as possible. I share my story. I share that making that decision to start a relationship with Jesus is the best decision I ever made, but my life has been hard. God's plans for us are good, but they don't always feel good. Life with Jesus is a great decision, but it's hard. I lay it all out, and then I let them decide. You should see their faces when I tell them nobody can decide for them, that it's their choice. Their faces light up with both wonder and a little fear. It's a powerful and overwhelming thing when you realize you can make your own choice.

I refuse to play soft music or dim the lights. I look them square in the eye and ask them to make their own choice. What results is usually unbelievably precious. What doesn't happen is a sea of hands in the air, a ripple effect crying, or rote repetition of prayer. What does happen is a handful of kids who make the well thought out and very personal choice to start a relationship with Jesus. I give them a general idea of how or what to pray and then I let them go from there. Little hands are held open in a show of surrender and hearts turn to Jesus. It's incredible. I've seen over and over again through the years that those kids who make the informed choice to follow Jesus point back to that point as the time it all started. They got it, and it left them changed.

When you give a child a choice, their timing is very rarely your timing.

I remember one 11-year-old girl name Lexi coming up to me and saying, "Miss Mel, I've decided to wait to start a relationship with Jesus. I feel like I want to sin a little more before I'm ready." The honesty of that statement blew me away. In the spirit of honesty, I was completely horrified. I also was thinking, "They didn't teach me what to say to THAT in college!" I realized I had a choice to make. I could guilt her and force her or I could release her.

I told her I was so glad she was being honest with me. I reminded her what was at stake and told her to let me know when she was ready. She made the decision about two years later. I had moved away, but she sent me a Facebook message to tell me she had finally decided to start a relationship with

Jesus. That girl is on fire for Jesus to this day. She waited until she was ready and she hasn't looked back once.

At one of my camps, a 10-year-old girl and her friend knocked on the door of my speaker room one morning. They came in to tell me that she had just decided to start a relationship with Jesus the night before. I was speechless. I hadn't talked about that choice for a couple of nights. In fact, I had just been beating myself up over what I felt had been a weak message the previous night. But this girl was beaming at me. BEAMING. She had come to see me a couple of days before and had been pretty sullen and quiet. She'd actually been on my heart because I had sensed something was going on within her. Now she stood in my room beaming at me with a glorious light in her eyes. I asked her what happened, and she explained that she had been lying in bed the night before thinking about what I had been talking about, and she decided she was ready to choose to start a relationship with Jesus. She had prayed and that was it. "Miss Mel, I woke up this morning and I feel so different. I can't stop smiling. I'm so happy... so joyful. I'm so glad I chose to make this decision. It changes everything. It all makes sense now. I get it. He loves me, He really loves me!" Those were her words and they were completely genuine. No one had told her to feel different or told her what to say. God was at work in her life because she made a choice.

That's the power of kids understanding they get to choose.

Let's take it further. Let's not raise and train kids to be victims of "I couldn't help myself," and "I didn't know," and "He made me do it." That's where our world is taking them; let's take them a different direction. Let's take them away from victimization, entitlement, and apathy and towards the fruit of the Spirit.

Realizing that you have the power to choose and that because of this power, you have to own your decisions, changes the way you make choices. Kids can handle that kind of power.

When we pass on faith and raise up kids who understand, as a part of their foundation, that they have the power to make wise choices, we change their future. They are equipped and aware. They become teenagers and young adults who understand that their choices affect themselves and the people around them, and they understand that the God who loves them allows them to make choices. The power to choose is a powerful thing that forever changes who you are.

Here are some examples of choices that kids can and get to make. (I always teach that it's a *privilege* to make choices.)

You get to choose your words. Talk about how your words to someone can make or break their day. How words can build you up or take you down. Refer back to Pineapple People. Your words can poke or they can heal.

"We all make many mistakes, but those who control their tongues can also control themselves in every other way. We can make a large horse turn around and go wherever we want by means of a small bit in its mouth. And a tiny rudder makes a huge ship turn wherever the pilot wants it to go, even though the winds are strong. So also, the tongue is a small thing, but what enormous damage it can do. A tiny spark can set a great forest on fire. And the tongue is a flame of fire. It is full of wickedness that can ruin your whole life. It can turn the entire course of your life into a blazing flame of destruction, for it is set on fire by hell itself. People can tame all kinds of animals and birds and reptiles and fish, but no one can tame the tongue. It is an uncontrollable evil, full of deadly poison. Sometimes it praises our Lord and Father, and sometimes it breaks out into curses against those who have been made in the image of God" (James 3:2–9).

You get to choose to point to Jesus with your life. Talk about how you live. Your life either points to Jesus or away. The choices you make matter to the people around you. Honor God with your life. When you allow God to be in charge of your life, you look different.

"But when the Holy Spirit controls our lives, He will produce this kind of fruit in us: love, joy, peace, patience, kindness, goodness, faithfulness, gentleness, and self-control. Here there is no conflict with the law. Those who belong to Christ Jesus have nailed the passions and desires of their sinful nature to his cross and crucified them there. If we are living now by the Holy Spirit, let us follow the Holy Spirit's leading in every part of our lives. Let us not become conceited, or irritate one another, or be jealous of one another" (Galatians 5:22–26).

You get to choose to forgive. Talk about how life is hard and people will hurt us. How we respond to those people is our choice, as is how we treat the people around us. Refer back to Pineapple People. Most people who hurt us need us to love them and show them the forgiveness that we have been given. Tell the story of Joseph.

"You have heard the law that says, 'Love your neighbor' and hate your enemy. But I say, love your enemies! Pray for those who persecute you! In that way, you will be acting as true children of your Father in heaven. For He gives His sunlight to both the evil and the good, and He sends rain on the just and the unjust alike. If you love only those who love you, what reward is there for that? Even corrupt tax collectors do that much. If you are kind only to your friends, how are you different from anyone else? Even pagans do that" (Matthew 5:43–47).

You get to choose to trust that God's plans for you are good, even when they don't feel good. This is a big one for kids. Because they are so literal, it's hard for them to grasp that His plans are good and leave it at that. They go home and dad's in jail, mom's sick, their dog died, and His plans don't look good at all. I like to add the "even when they don't feel good." It resonates with kids and makes sense in their minds. Share a personal story and talk about your own journey with trusting.

You get to choose your friends and the kind of friend you are. You can use a number of Bible stories for this. David's buddy (as I call him) is one of my favorites. You know, the other shepherd who chose to watch David's sheep so he could go to his brothers. Him being a good friend ultimately allowed David to take care of Goliath. Define the kind of friends kids need around them, or better yet, have them help you make a list.

You get to choose your attitude. Try telling the story of Daniel in the lion's den from a completely different perspective. Not only will kids love hearing it a new way, you'll go deeper with them as you help them see the different attitudes chosen. Darius chose pride, the other advisors chose jealousy, and Daniel chose faithfulness. Other people's poor choices may affect us, but we still get to choose our attitudes.

CHAPTER 8

W E NEED TO PASS on faith and raise up kids who have had an encounter with Jesus and know His voice. I was six years old in my room memorizing a verse for our church group. In the midst of memorizing Romans 3:10 about no one doing good, no not one, God began stirring in my heart. My little six-year-old brain put together that if no one did good, that meant everyone sinned and was doomed. And if they didn't know Jesus, I knew that meant they would go to hell. It broke my heart to think of all the people in the world who would die without knowing Jesus if we didn't tell them. God spoke to my heart and I knew I was supposed to be a missionary. I had heard His voice and I knew it was Him.

I was 11 years old and I knew things weren't quite right at our church and with my family. Things were changing and shifting. As much as I didn't like it, I knew it was happening. Deep in my heart I began preparing myself to move away from the place that had been home since I was five. I didn't know what was going on, but I knew something was about to change. When my parents sat my sisters and me down and told us we were going to move, I was prepared, and I knew it was God who had been speaking to my heart.

MISSING

I was 15 and sitting forlornly on the front porch swing waiting for the mailman. I was anticipating and hoping for a letter from the boy I had met on a mission's trip over the summer. He was the first boy to call me pretty, and I liked him. Swinging back and forth I was anxiously searching the streets for any glimpse of the mailman when I heard an audible voice say to me, "Don't you know, I am enough for you? I love you, Melissa." My swinging stopped and I swung around looking for who had spoken to me while my eyes filled with tears as I realized I knew that voice and I knew that message. It was God and I knew it was Him speaking exactly what I needed to hear.

Can you remember the first time you heard God's voice? It may have been a shift in your heart, an audible voice, a song on the radio just when you needed it, or a verse that seemed to have been written just for you. Whatever it was and whenever it was, I bet you remember. It's pretty hard to forget when the God of the universe speaks to you. Suddenly all of the stories and verses become real and you realize the whole relationship thing actually means there is someone on the other end. It's powerful and unforgettable.

In Barna's research he lists "facilitate connection with Jesus" as one of the ways you can help Millennials stay connected to the church. By helping facilitate a deeper sense of intimacy with God, we can help Millennials stay connected to a church community. He goes on to explain, "For example, Millennials who remain active are more likely than those who dropped out to say they believe Jesus speaks to them personally in a way that is real and relevant (68 versus 25 percent)." You don't forget a Jesus that is real, relevant, and relational. It changes you.

I had a relationship with Jesus when I went to college, but in many ways it was all on my terms. It was when I had time, when I felt like it, and it was all about me. The idea of listening for God and tuning my ear to His voice was convicting to me, but I rarely took the time, or knew how to make time, to actually allow Him to speak. I thrived on being busy, sociable, and occupied.

I became an RA (resident assistant) my sophomore year. In August the whole RA staff went away for a week of training, team building, and soul care in preparation for the school year. One afternoon we were told to take three hours with God. THREE HOURS! I was sure I had misunderstood. Much to my dismay I had heard correctly. We were to take our Bibles and journals, find a comfortable secluded spot, and spend time with Jesus.

I remember I found a spot looking out at the beautiful lake our cabin sat on in northern Minnesota. I gave it my very best for the first 20 minutes. I prayed, waited, prayed some more, and nothing happened. The next 20 minutes I groaned and complained. The 20 minutes after that I doodled. The hour after that I read my Bible and journaled random thoughts in my head. I wrote down hopes I had for the year, prayers I was praying for my floor of girls, frustrations I had had with my summer, etc. In the last hour I had finally shut up and given up enough to actually listen for God. I finally got out of my own way, and God began to speak to me. I spent the next hour journaling what he was laying on my heart, messages He was giving me, and wisdom He was bestowing upon me. It was beautiful. It was also exhausting. However, hearing God speak to me like that—and realizing if I shut up and truly listened for Him and waited on Him, He would speak—was life changing.

What followed was a dedication to making time to hear from God a regular part of my spiritual disciplines. While I still have to give myself time to quiet down and listen, I've gotten better at it. It comes easier. It's been a learned process, but it's been a vital part of who I am as a believer. I've found space on beaches all around the world, beside rivers in the mountains, in front of roaring fireplaces in cabins in the woods, and even on a wooden dock on the Danube in Vienna, Austria. Wherever I have lived, wherever I have gone, I've made space to hear from God. It's become a part of who I am.

When I became a children's pastor, I very much wanted to help train my kiddos to hear from God and to make space for Him. I wanted to go beyond simple devotions to actually hearing from and responding to God. It was such a painfully slow learning process for me as an adult, I wanted to instill that into their foundation as children. I didn't know, however, if one could do that. I am thankful that God created me in such a way that the unknown has never been a problem for me. It's always been an opportunity.

After praying and considering what it might all look like, I took a leap of faith and scheduled an overnight retreat with my fourth, fifth, and sixth graders. At the time I was ministering in a church in northern Idaho. I booked us at a rustic retreat center along the Snake River. Our team of five adults took 15 preteens into the wilderness for a 24-hour period for Encounter.

I had a wonderful team of leaders who not only supported me but trusted me, even though I'm sure they had their doubts. Our first afternoon we had carved out time for what we called "deep thoughts." I rang the bell and all the kids came running into our meeting area. I explained to them that they were going to have some time alone with God. There were no rules other than they weren't allowed to talk to anyone else or be near anyone else, and they had to stay within site of the main building. This was time between them and God. I gave them all journals to accompany their Bibles and a sheet of simple questions and thoughts to guide them. I explained to them that when the time was up, I would ring the bell and we would go on to game time. There was much cheering for the promised game time and their favorite game, Capture the Flag.

I sent them all on their way with a smile and as much bravado as I could muster. I put on my leader face, you know the face, the one that says, "This is going to be great, and you're going to love it." It's the face that hides that you're thinking, *This is probably going to fail. I don't think you can do this with kids. What was I thinking?* They all ran out and I dropped to my chair with my head in my hands and prayed that it would work.

The difference between boys and girls is hilarious to me. After pleading for the Lord to "make it work," I went out to check on them. Girls had grabbed blankets and their stuffed animals and even a snack or two and had set up house on different areas on the lawn. They were snuggled down in their cocoons reading their Bibles. The boys were a whole other story. One was perched on top of a rock staring off into the distance. Another one was hanging upside down from a tree reading his Bible. The beautiful thing was they were all quiet, and they all seemed to be engrossed in what they were doing.

I kept a careful eye on them and a careful eye on my watch. I didn't want to go any longer than I had told them. I wasn't sure if what we had done would be a win, but I was planning on making sure I held up my end of the bargain. After exactly 15 minutes, I rang the bell and stood at the door waiting for the kids. Honestly, I expected a noisy stampede to get ready for Capture the Flag. I was completely shocked as the kids slowly began to leave their spots and amble toward me. One by one they reached me and one by one they said, "I wasn't done yet Miss Mel, I wanted more time. I wasn't done hearing from God." Every. Single. Kid.

That was the first time I realized we were onto something. The next day the kids had another "deep thoughts" time and again they came back saying they wanted more time. I even had kids asking if they could use their free time to spend time with God. Umm, yeah! I was blown away.

The next year our retreat went to two nights with two 30-minute "deep thoughts" sessions each day. Every time kids asked for more time. They were journaling, praying, reading their Bibles, and hearing from God. They were being deeply affected by their time with God. They would share what God was saying to them, and it was deep and real. They encountered God and were not the same.

Recently, while writing this book, I sat down with a group of kids who were a part of Encounter. They are now either high school seniors or have graduated. We began reminiscing about Encounter. First of all, they loved it and some of their best childhood memories had taken place there. Second of all, their favorite part of it had been "deep thoughts." They were all talking about how because of that they now journal, know how to hear from God, recognize His voice, understand they're a part of something bigger, and love Jesus. Junior high and high school were certainly not easy, but they knew Jesus and it made a difference.

When you, as an adult, hear God's voice, it changes you and you don't forget it. When a child hears God's voice, it makes an imprint into the very core of who they are. They do not forget it. It changes them.

A word of caution for you. Our job as the adults in these kids' lives is to do four things when it comes to kids knowing and encountering God's voice.

Explain. Explain what encountering God's voice might be like. I always explain they may feel something in their hearts, they might see a picture, they might hear a song, they might notice something in a Bible verse, and they might hear an audible voice. Give multiple ways they may encounter God.

Anticipate and expect. Anticipate that God will speak to kids and expect it to happen. Do not underestimate how God will work through kids.

Be quiet. Hush. Shh. Stop talking. This is about them and God, not about you and your words. Explain briefly and succinctly and then let them go. Be quiet; leave space for God to talk. Shh!

Don't judge. Don't judge how or what a child hears from God. It may not look or sound like you would expect it to, but that does not mean it's not from God. The important thing is that they encounter God, not that you completely understand it. Listen with pleasure as they tell their stories and thank God with them that He spoke to them.

I wrote this on my Facebook page last summer:

I believe God talks to kids and I believe in letting kids know that. Tonight during chapel at the camp I'm speaking at, I did what I always do. I told the kids to quietly prepare their hearts for God to speak to them. After chapel, a little eight-year-old girl came up to me. These were her words: "Miss Mel, I started a relationship with God a while ago but I haven't really been talking to Him. When you told us to listen for God, I heard the sounds of rocks tumbling. I could picture Jesus picking me up out of the rocks." And then she just beamed at me. And that, my kidmin friends, is why we do what we do. That girl met Jesus in a very real way that night. God speaks to kids. Don't be afraid of it, try to avoid it, or stay unaware. Embrace it and allow God to move. He will.

At another camp, I had a nine-year-old boy come up to me after time alone with God so excited to share with me what God had said to him. "Miss Mel, I was standing in the grass over there. I was standing because I didn't feel like sitting."

"No problem, that's fine. Go on."

"Well I was reading about the ascension of our Lord Jesus Christ when the clouds above me moved open and the sun came out and it shined right on me! Right on me! It shined on me and I knew it was God! I knew He was speaking to me!"

I gave that kid the biggest high five and told him I was so glad he knew God had spoken to him. As he ran off I wanted to judge his whole sunbeam experience. My adultness wanted to tell him that was simply the clouds moving and not God speaking to him. My adultness wanted to ask him what God had actually said to him other than the sun shining on him. My adultness wanted to judge, and box, and control, and interpret. God not so gently whispered in my ear that it was not at all about me and completely about him. I was convicted. Who was I to judge what someone else heard from God? All I knew was that that boy was giddy with excitement over his encounter with God. It had impacted him and that's what mattered.

The number two reason Barna lists for why Millennials leave the church is because "teens' and twentysomethings' experience of Christianity is shallow." God is boring and/or irrelevant. A God who has been encountered in a real and personal way is neither boring nor shallow. He's real, relational, and relevant. When a child has a heart encounter and connection with Jesus, it changes them. It imprints onto their very foundation, and they are never the same. It's hard to turn your back on a God that you've heard, known, and encountered.

We need to pass on faith and raise up kids who have had an encounter with Jesus and know how to hear His voice.

YOU

This is about to get uncomfortable. We've spent a good chunk of this book talking about kids and what they need from us. I hope you've been challenged and inspired. For the most part, however, I'm guessing it's been a "comfortable" challenged and inspired. Now it gets awkward. Now we talk about you. Yes, you. The adult reading this book. Whether you have kids, work with kids, love kids, know kids, or tolerate kids, I'm talking about you.

Here's the deal. We wouldn't have lost a generation and be losing the next one if we as adults had been doing a stellar job. Programming and curriculum can only be blamed so far. The fact is curriculum and programming is only as good as the person teaching it and leading it. If we have to rethink how we reach and raise kids, we have to turn the mirror on ourselves and admit it's time for a change.

As the adults in kids' lives, we are the face of Jesus to them. Like it or not, their view of who God is directly links to the adults in their lives. By the age of five, a child's lifelong view of God is formed. Scientists will tell you that this view is irreversible. I always like to say that those scientists obviously don't know the God we serve, the God who is constantly writing a new story for us and who is in the business of creating beauty out of ashes. Yes, God is gracious to redeem and rewrite, but the reality is, kids are significantly impacted by the adults in their lives. That ought to have us rethinking who we are, whom we recruit, and the message we live.

This next section is going to talk about what kids need from the adults in their lives. It's time we step up and out and pass on faith in ways we never expected.

I told you this would get uncomfortable. You can't say I didn't warn you.

CHAPTER 9

KIDS NEED ADULTS IN THEIR lives who love Jesus. I know that may sound trite, but it's true. A love for Jesus is the first and most important thing I look for when I'm recruiting people. Funny enough, a love for kids is not the most important thing. I want people who are passionately sold out in love with Jesus. I can work from there.

I travel extensively working with churches providing consultation and training. At every single church I go into, I find people who love kids and are desiring to find ways to teach them and reach them more effectively. Unfortunately, in a large percentage of the churches I've visited, at least one or more of their regular weekly volunteers does not have a personal relationship with Jesus. I know that sounds crazy, but it's true. I got over my surprise long ago when the pastor or children's director would call me a few weeks after my time with them and tell me that so-and-so was teaching third and fourth grade "and didn't even know the Lord!" That is not uncommon.

In fact, my guess is that if you are reading this and you're in a leadership position in ministry to children, you most likely have one or more regular main volunteers who do not have a relationship with Jesus. They are teaching about a God they don't even know.

How does this happen? No other ministry in the church requires as many volunteers as children's ministry. We need to maintain a safe adult to child ratio and we need to maintain control. That equates to the fact that we need bodies. Typically once a person has gone through training and a background check, as long as they like kids, we'll take them.

Unlike kids, adults are good at choosing their words wisely. They know how to fill out the application and make it seem like they have a relationship with Jesus. Most often, they think they do, and are not purposely trying to deceive. What happens to us is we get so busy trying to get everything staffed that we don't necessarily take the time to read carefully. If we don't watch for phrases such as, "Well I guess I've always known the Lord," "I've attended church my whole life," "I grew up as a Christian," "I've always been a Christian," or "I have a strong belief in God," we may be missing out on some important clues into their spiritual walks. And honestly, we are so desperate for teachers, that kind of language can sound "good enough." Shame on us.

Do not hear me disqualifying non-Christians from serving in children's ministry. I can always find a place for anyone, and I have. From the mom with the record to the elderly couple who is "done with kids" to the man who is just there because his kids are, and even to the youth doing community service, I have found places for people who are willing to serve.

Not everyone, however, will directly interact with and teach kids. Our kids' spiritual journeys and foundations are too important. That mom with a record ran media for me and had no actual contact with kids. That elderly couple took over our hospitality team for our family service. That man ran sound for me and found Jesus as a result of learning alongside the kids. And that youth worked for me during the week on cleaning and organizing projects. I found places for each one of them and they flourished in their spots. However, none of them were the right fit for actual interaction with kids.

Kids are observant. They are always watching. They learn by watching and by modeling. I want kids modeling themselves after teachers and team members who love Jesus and have a real, vibrant relationship with Him. It's crucial to me. I would rather stop a program, close the preschool room, and turn parents away than staff my program with people who don't know the Lord or aren't walking with Him. It's that important to me. (Please note that we're looking for people who are in love with Jesus and are walking closely with Him. I know a lot of Christians who are not exhibiting much fruit in their lives. Seek out and utilize people sold out for Jesus who walk daily with Him.)

When we look at this through the lens of building a foundation, we cannot ignore the importance of having kids be impacted by people who love Jesus and know him. It is not enough to know *how* to teach, we must have personal knowledge of *who* we are teaching about. The God of the stories, the silly crafts, and the songs is the very same God who formed the universe, who delicately knit together each and every child in your class. He's a jealous God who longs for a relationship with those little ones. He is the ultimate teacher, convictor, and lover. Our job is to point to him in everything we say and do. We must have teachers and adults involved in kids' lives and ministry whose lives point to Jesus. They must know Him in order to impact little hearts with Him.

One step further is this: if you love Jesus, tell your face. I am constantly amazed at the number of Christians I meet who look like some of the most miserable people on earth. Their very countenances speak of misery, defeat, and agony. What surprises me further is that when I talk to them, they know the Lord and love Him. I want to shout, "Then tell your face!" Little eyes are watching and wondering and drawing conclusions. It is hard to make a connection between someone who says they know Jesus and someone who always looks miserable. That doesn't connect in a kid's mind.

I recruited Jeff and his wife Kelly to serve in our VBS program. Jeff is a mechanic and definitely a man's man. His wife is a sweetheart. I always like to recruit couples, and I knew I wanted them specifically for one of our rowdier age groups. I wanted Jeff because I needed another man in that group, but I also knew he loved Jesus. I put Jeff and his wife with our first and second graders. They had their hands full wrangling and corralling all of our busy little ones.

The boys especially, had attitudes and were very active. They looked up to Jeff, though, as if he was some kind of hero. That explains why they were watching him during large group worship time. They noticed that he had his eyes closed and when tears started appearing on his face, they began whispering to each other and nudging each other. When Jeff continued to cry, one of the boys finally leaned over to him and said, "Why are you crying?"

Jeff looked at Him with all sincerity and with tears in his eyes and said, "I love Jesus and when we sing about Him and how good He is, I sometimes cry. It's okay for men to cry." Then Jeff turned back around and continued to worship the God he loved. Those little boys continued to watch Jeff and they began to pay more attention to the words of the songs and the God of the songs. They were impacted. Jeff impacted those boys in a deep way. He loved Jesus and was not afraid to show it or say it or act on it. I guarantee you those boys don't remember our theme for that VBS, but they remember Mr. Jeff who loved Jesus enough to cry tears of joy.

CHAPTER 10

KIDS NEED HEALTHY ADULTS. Now I'm not referring to physical health, although we do need physically healthy adults to work with kids in our ministry. I'm talking about something deeper here. I'm talking about spiritual, emotional, and mental health.

Now please don't think for a minute that God can't use you if you aren't perfectly healthy. We all know that's not true. God is in the business of using the broken and the weak for His glory. There is an important difference here between adults who are striving towards health and adults who are comfortable in their lack of health. Kids need to see adults who are striving towards health.

When we approach recruiting people to work with kids, we need to look for health. By the way, striving towards health is a piece of health in and of itself.

I know I'm biased when I say that working with kids is the best ministry in the world. I love it! I love kids. There is nothing like walking into a room of kids and getting hugs and love. I find joy in a child wrapping their arms around me and saying they are so glad to see me. I take delight in knowing kids want to be around me and want to spend time with me. I do not, however, find my total fulfillment in any of these things. I do not find my sense of self-worth. I do not find my identity. Kids are precious to me but they are not my everything.

See the difference? It's subtle, but it's important. I think we've made a mistake in children's ministry through the years. We have allowed unhealthy people to help shape our kid's spiritual lives. I know this may seem like I'm stepping on a few toes, but bear with me.

Many people find their security, self-worth, safety, and fulfillment in ministering to kids. That should scare you; that should sound an alarm bell within you. That is not okay.

Adults need to spend at least part of their time with other adults. Fellowship, accountability, and growth must happen with other adults. Nothing concerns me more than going into a church and hearing about volunteers who have never taken a break, who haven't made it to "big church" in years, and who have created their own little kingdom in their kids' ministry room. WARNING! That's an indicator of poor health. It is easy to escape real life and hide away with kids.

It was the first night of VBS. I was the director and connecting with everyone and giving out clipboards and running around. I had heard a rumor that something might not be quite right with one of my storytellers, but I hadn't heard anything beyond that. Laura found me 30 minutes before we started. She proceeded to tell me she didn't feel right about serving in a storyteller capacity that week. She told me, "I'm sleeping with my boyfriend and I'm not repentant." Those were her exact words.

A hundred different things ran through my mind. I was concerned with the major gap I now had in my storyteller spot, I was concerned with what I was going to do, and I was a little bit mad I was just now finding everything out. Then I looked at Laura. Her lips were quivering and her downcast eyes were full of tears. She was ashamed and she was scared. I wrapped my arms around her and told her I loved her. I calmly explained to her that she was loved and forgiven. I told her due to her current choices, I could not have her in a major teaching role, but I still wanted her help that week. I prayed over her and reiterated that we were a church who accepted her where she was at.

Laura graciously moved into crafts and while she allowed her shame to keep her away the rest of the week, she was shown love. She came back to church that Sunday and attended regularly until she moved away.

It was an incredibly hard thing for me to do from a personal perspective and a programming perspective, but I cared more about having a healthy adult teaching our kids God's Word than I did about the hole I had to fill at the last minute. Our associate pastor and I ended up filling the storyteller role. We had ten kids start relationships with Jesus. We believe God honored that hard decision.

Strive for health. Pass on faith not by having it all together, but by striving for more and more of Jesus.

CHAPTER 11

KIDS NEED ADULTS WHO are willing to get a little uncomfortable. Let's be completely honest in this chapter. Working with kids can be uncomfortable.

There's the physical side of it. The tiny chairs we have to delicately balance our adult bodies on with our knees up by our ears. The tiny little toys that seem to lie in wait until our shoes come off. The snacks that are indeed portioned for a tiny person and only leave us hungrier. Then there is the reality that when you're the adult leader in a room full of kids and helpers, you have to keep going no matter what.

On one particular Sunday I was standing by the door in our large group room welcoming all of our teachers and kiddos. I was the large group leader so I was "on." Unfortunately I had yet to learn the very important lesson of feeding myself properly on a Sunday morning. One minute I was greeting kids and starting to feel a little woozy, and the next thing I knew I was lying on the couch in the library being force fed stale goldfish crackers. I hadn't completely blacked out, but I had scared the kids and my volunteers. All I knew was I had to get enough of those crackers in me to bring the blood sugar up so I could go teach. Talk about uncomfortable.

Then there is the emotional side of it that's uncomfortable. How does a child know just what insecure button to push? How do they know to hit you right at your lowest, most vulnerable point?

One Sunday I walked into church feeling particularly snazzy. I had just gotten my hair cut, and while I wasn't completely sure about it, I had decided to embrace it. Wouldn't you know it, one of my fifth grade boys noticed me immediately. He gave me a long steady look and then shook his head sadly, "Oh Miss Mel, that's not good, it's not good at all."

Uncomfortable.

For as much love, laughter, and hugs kids give out, they give just as much attitude, brutal honesty, and drama. It's not comfortable working with them, but it's rewarding.

Kids need us as adults to be willing to be uncomfortable. That uncomfortableness can come in many different ways. It may come in the form of physical or emotional discomfort. It also may come in the form of us taking a step into their world for the purpose of loving and serving them better. That's the type of uncomfortable I want to focus on here.

For too long we have allowed ourselves to live in a comfort bubble. It's the bubble of assuming that we know what kids need and what they're dealing with. I haven't seen this with people who work with any other age group. Youth pastors work hard to stay aware of a teenager's world. Pastors to young adults are constantly doing research and working on awareness. Even those who teach pastors and senior pastors work hard to stay in touch with their audience. Why do those of us who work with kids not do the same?

I can't say I have the answer for why we don't enter more fully into kids' worlds, but my hunch is because it's uncomfortable. A kid in today's world is dealing with stuff that is far heavier and deeper than even I would like to admit. The reality is, though, that it is their reality. We must be aware of their reality so we can better love them and minister to them. But, it is uncomfortable.

I'm sure I'm not alone in longing for the days of *Leave it to Beaver* and even *Happy Days*. I long for my kid's biggest problems to be finding their lost bike, fighting with their sibling over setting the table, and trying to figure out how to tell mom about her broken lamp. I wish those were the types of problems kids today are struggling with. That's not the case.

- Fewer than 10 percent of families in North America have one or more family dinners together per week.

- Sixty percent of the 18 and under crowd in the cell phone market use smart phones.

- Kids spend 7 hours and 38 minutes on average a day consuming media.

- By the age of 14, twenty-five percent of kids will have been the victim of "sexting."

- Twenty-six percent of US children live in single-parent homes.

- Eating disorders have been on the rise for the past three decades and have been increasing more rapidly in boys and ethnic minorities.

- The largest group of Internet pornography consumers is between 12 and 17 years old.

- Forty-three percent of children growing up in America today are being raised without their biological fathers.[3]

- Seventy-five percent of children with divorced parents live with their mothers.[4]

- A child with a biological mother who is living with a man who is not the child's father is 33 times more likely to suffer abuse.[5]

- At least 676,569 children, or almost 1 in every 100 children in the United States, were abused in 2011.[6]

- When surveyed, 7.6 percent of third graders and 12.7 percent of ninth graders admitted to engaging in what researchers call nonsuicidal self-injury.[7]

These are just some of the startling statistics I could have pulled for this chapter. Statistics are just statistics until they take the form of the story, until they become personal. Those are the statistics; now here are some real life stories.

---

3. *http://www.children-and-divorce.com/children-divorce-statistics.html*

4. *http://www.mckinleyirvin.com/blog/divorce/32-shocking-divorce-statistics/*

5. Dreamcatchers for Abused Children, *http://www.drphil.com/articles/article/727*

6. *http://pediatrics.about.com/od/childabuse/a/05_abuse_stats.htm*

7. *http://www.nbcnews.com/health/cutting-compulsion-affects-kids-young-7-study-finds-822700*

After one evening speaking at camp, I was sitting in the snack area when an eleven-year-old girl came up to me. She sat across from me, rolled up her sleeves, and said, "Miss Mel, I've been doing this and I don't know why." She had scars and fresh cuts all up her arms.

A ten-year-old boy came up to me in angry tears. "Miss Mel, I'm worried about my parents. I think they're going to be divorced when I get home. Dad has a big spending problem; he can't stop using credit cards. Mom yells at him, but he only remembers not to use the cards when I'm there to remind him. I've been at camp all week, and I know he's forgotten, and they're going to be divorced."

A twelve-year-old boy told me about the fights his parents were having. He told me how his father would yell at him and call him a mistake and a loser. "I have a gun under my bed and sometimes I hold it up to my face and pray I'll have the courage to pull the trigger."

An eight-year-old girl told me she wasn't allowed to see her grandpa anymore because he had been touching her inappropriately. She didn't understand and missed her grandpa.

A six-year-old foster child would come to Sunday School and get so angry he would bang his head against the wall and say, "I wish you were dead, I wish I was dead!"

An eight-year-old boy had to be physically removed from our mid-week program by his father and a medical professional and was taken to the emergency room after threatening to hurt himself and the people around him.

A twelve-year-old girl called me six hours after her father shot and killed her mother and then shot and killed himself while she was in the basement.

Each of those statistics is a story and a child and each one is heartbreaking. It's heartbreaking and it's uncomfortable. Sometimes I wish I could place my fingers in my ears and say "la la la la!" at the top of my lungs so I don't have to hear their stories. It would be easier. Honestly, there are days I have to brace myself for what I'm going to hear. It's uncomfortable.

Here's the deal, I don't think God sacrificed His Son, saved us from certain death, and gave us the greatest gift of all time so that we could live in our comfort zones. If we're serious about being Jesus to a dying world, it's going to be uncomfortable at times. If we're serious about changing the 4/14 Window and changing what their future is going to look like, we're going to have to be willing to get a little uncomfortable.

Kids need adults in their lives who are willing to enter into their reality. When that 12-year-old girl called me to tell me about the death of her parents, I didn't know what to do. I didn't have words or a strategy or any idea what she needed. I was so far out of my depth. She called me and immediately started sobbing. I did the only thing I knew to do, I listened and cried along with her. It was uncomfortable.

When I flew out to see her a month after her parent's death, and I took her and two other girls on a weekend retreat to help her process, I had no idea what to do. I was fighting a massive sob fest every time I looked at her. I had scoured my textbooks and blogs for any idea of how to handle a murder/suicide, and I had found nothing. So I let her talk, I helped her journal, I listened to her process, and I cried with her. I was uncomfortable.

When I took that girl "home" to her grandma's trailer, and she had me take a detour by her house where the shooting had happened, I was wrecked inside. She had me peek in windows and pointed out where the tragedy had happened. She showed me her family's boat, her mom's flowers, and her backyard. By the time I dropped her off with her grandma where she was sleeping on the couch, my hands were shaking with grief. When she clung to me and sobbed her heart out as I was leaving, all I could do was hug her. And when I was finally alone I curled into a ball and wept until I had no tears left. I was uncomfortable.

As the months and now years have gone by and I have journeyed with that girl, it has been uncomfortable. I've lost hours of sleep as God has woken me up in the night to intercede on her behalf. I've cried more tears than I can count. I've used vacation time to spend time loving on her. One moment in particular I cried out to God in exhaustion and defeat asking Him if I could please be done. In His lovingkindness, He whispered to my heart, "Everyone is fighting against her, I'm calling you to fight for her." Loving people the way God calls us to love them is uncomfortable. Loving kids and entering into their reality is uncomfortable.

In Barna's research about Millennials he says, "When comparing twentysomethings who remained active in their faith beyond high school and twentysomethings who dropped out of church, the Barna study uncovered a significant difference between the two. Those who stay were twice as likely to have a close personal friendship with an adult inside the church. He goes on to say that, "Seven out of ten Millennials who dropped out of church did *not* have a close friendship with an adult."[8]

If we're truly going to reach this 4/14 Window and prevent another Millennial crisis, it's going to require intentional

---

8. *https://www.barna.org/barna-update/millennials/635-5-reasons-millennials-stay-connected-to-church#. UlR6amTF3Cc*

adults who are willing to be a little uncomfortable. It's going to take you passing on faith and being willing to enter into a kid's world, in the muck and the mess, and love them and point them to Jesus.

CHAPTER 12

KIDS NEED AUTHENTIC ADULTS. I talked earlier about the great need for authenticity. In a world that celebrates "reality" stars, has "photoshopped" filters built into every camera app that are readily available for every picture taken, and allows the media to define normal, there seems to be little room for authenticity. And yet, that is what this generation is crying out for.

I spend a week every summer meeting with international workers who have just returned back to the US after serving overseas for four years. My job is to reacquaint them with the American kid. They usually have a number of presuppositions about American kids based on what media tells them or what some cranky blog has told them. I love encouraging them and helping them rethink American kids. American kids can sit still, and they do love to ask questions. Their attention spans are short, but can easily be lengthened with a good story, and their hearts are open to Jesus and people. One thing that is new with this culture of kids is their attitude towards adults.

Back in the not so long ago day, kids respected adults and listened to them because they were adults. It was kind of a given.

This generation of kids is completely different. They don't care who you are. They will not listen to you or respect you until they know you. It's based on relationship and a connection. While I certainly don't love this new trend, I do think it's a wonderful open door for us to step through as adults who want to impact kids. Kids want to know us. What a great opportunity!

Feel free to refer back to the previous chapter if you find this idea uncomfortable. Kids need and want us to be vulnerable with them and share our stories. That's how they get to know us and in turn why they choose to respect us. They're looking for a point of connection, they're looking for a spot of real life, and they're desperate to see if we're for real. I personally believe there is a myth out there that says relevancy is the most important thing when dealing with kids. Wrong! Being real matters far more than being relevant.

When I speak at camps, I'm usually brand new to every kid and adult in the room. I've got hundreds of pairs of eyes staring at me daring me to prove myself worthy of their time and attention. No pressure, right? Yikes. Long ago I decided it was only fair to kids that if I was going to talk to them for an extended amount of time and they were going to listen to me, I would first listen to them. Later, as I began to understand the need for kids to get to know me before they respect me, that idea of allowing them to talk first became even more important. So while every eye is staring me down, I start with about one minute of who I am, and then I tell them it's their turn to ask anything they want to know about me. I explain that before I talk, every single time they will be allowed to ask any question they want of me.

It doesn't take long before hands shoot up and the questions start coming. They usually start fairly shallow early in the week. "What's your favorite color?" and "Are you married?" (Inevitably when I answer this question with a "no," some sweet little boy will offer to marry me.)

I always take the opportunity to share a personal story when I answer at least one of the questions. That encourages more questions, and by the end of the week I could spend my whole time sharing life stories.

Throughout the week, the questions get deeper, which tells me how much the kids want to understand me and see if I'm legit.

"Miss Mel, tell about a time you doubted God."

"Miss Mel, can you tell us about a time when you were the most hurt by a person?"

"Miss Mel, when was the last time you decided God wasn't worth it and you wanted to give up?"

Deep heartwrenching questions require deep soul-baring answers. As I answer, kids get to know me. As they get to know me, they trust me. As they trust me, they listen to me and respect me, and as they listen to me and respect me, they open up to me.

I have been in church after church where I see kids dying for someone to be open with them, desperately searching for someone safe enough to talk to about real life stuff. What I find so sad is that I can be in a church for one Sunday morning and share briefly and kids will start opening up to me. It's like the flood gates open when they finally find someone they can trust and talk to.

I was at one church out east where I was asked to share up front for about 15 minutes during the Sunday service. It was a rather conservative church that had brought me in specifically to help them assess why they weren't retaining families and kids from their large events. I immediately could pinpoint some issues and my knees were knocking in the pew right before I went up to speak. I knew anything I had to say about the importance of kids and families was going to fly in the face of what many of them believed and held to. I went up slowly praying the whole way. God in His kindness gently whispered in my ear, "Just do your thing." Not overly specific, but I knew what I was supposed to do.

I spoke for 15 minutes about the real life conditions of families and kids. I brought the real world into their church sanctuary for 15 minutes as I told them what was really going on and how desperately people need the church to step up and be the church as God designed it. I saw a couple shocked faces, but the majority of people were wiping tears, taking notes, and nodding their heads.

I headed right out the back doors of the sanctuary to go hang out and observe the kids once they were dismissed. The kids no sooner filed out before a 13-year-old girl in a sweet flowered dress asked to talk to me. She asked me, "Miss Mel, you talked about cutting up there, right?"

In my head I was thinking, "Pretty sure that's not what I was talking about and definitely not what my main point was." I simply nodded.

"I have some friends who are cutting themselves, and I've been thinking about doing it too." And like a flood her story came pouring out, and I couldn't have stopped her if I tried. "My dad tried to kill my mom, so he's in jail and doesn't live with us. My mom doesn't come to church, and she doesn't really care about God so my grandma brings me here. I lie in bed most nights and cry myself to sleep. Sometimes I put my pillow over my face and wish I could stop breathing so it would all go away."

This story so badly needed to spill out of her, we weren't even sitting down; I had just pulled her into a quiet corner in the room. The other kids couldn't hear her, but during her story I noticed the pastor's wife come near us and listen. When the little girl was done pouring out her story, the pastor's wife looked at me with tears in her eyes. I chatted with the girl, gave her a little advice, and more importantly connected her with an adult. The pastor's wife came up to me later and told me that girl had been coming to the church her entire life, and nobody knew her story. Nobody knew how on the edge she was, how deeply hurt she was. Surrounded by a church full of well-meaning people, she hadn't found one person who was safe and open enough to talk to until a random stranger walked up on stage and shared her heart.

It seems shocking, right? It may even seem like that's one of those stories that happens everywhere else but in your church community. You can think that if you want, if that makes you feel more comfortable, but the truth is that it is very likely in your church you have kids looking for authenticity, looking for adults they feel safe with so they can share real life with them, and they are not finding it.

Gone are the days where kids respect adults simply because they're their elders. My generation respected adults. We may have stuck our tongues out behind their backs, but we respected them. This generation of kids doesn't care who you are. It doesn't matter how much you command respect, you're not going to get it until you understand something very simple. Kids today are asking for something more. They're saying this,

"I don't respect you until I trust you, and I don't trust you until I know you." If you want kids to listen to you, you have to share of yourself. A louder voice and stricter rules will accomplish little when compared to authentic vulnerability. Allow kids to get to know you so they can trust you and respect you.

I was asked to speak to fourth through sixth graders at a winter retreat. This camp was in northern Minnesota in January so the theme was Avalanche. Churches from all over brought kids. Primarily the kids were church kids and involved in programs at the church.

I chose to focus on life's avalanches that take us by surprise and change the course we thought we were on. I started my chapel time with my regular question time and then moved into a personal story of my own, an avalanche in my life. It's important to note here that the story I shared was about a real and hurtful time in my life. I didn't overdramatize a pet dying or share a story off the Internet; I shared about a time in my life as an adult that an avalanche came and completely redirected my course. I shared about my anger, fear, and frustration. I was real with them.

After I shared, I encouraged them to share with me, or their leaders, about avalanches in their own lives. I let them know I'd be sitting in the snack area afterwards if they wanted to talk. That night blew me away. I had a line up of kids wanting to talk to me and share their avalanche stories. Child after child sat down across from me and broke my heart with their very hurtful and very raw avalanches. Because I had been vulnerable and authentic, they returned that to me. It opened door after door for me to connect them with one of their leaders and get them talking to an adult in their world. The adults were shocked by the stories they were hearing from their church kids, and they made me so proud as they willingly stepped up to listen, love, pray, and share their own stories.

Kids need authentic adults to do life with them. Life with Jesus is one of the hardest and best decisions ever, so live it out in front of them. Kids don't need the shined up and put together you, they need the authentic and real you. That is what makes a difference. Pass on faith, be vulnerable, be open, be you, be authentic, and be Jesus.

CHAPTER 13

KIDS NEED ADULTS WHO don't underestimate them. If we're going to empower kids to believe that they can change the world, we must first believe that to be true about them as well. Kids are amazing, they're a force, and God uses them.

I was seven years old when I led my first person to Christ. My family was camping, and I met a friend on the playground. She didn't know about Jesus, so I told her about Him and told her she should ask Him into her heart. She thought it seemed like a good idea, so we prayed together right there on the jungle gym with our legs wrapped around colorful monkey bars. After we prayed, we kept playing and I kept answering her questions about Jesus.

I'll never forget walking back into our campsite after being called for by my mom and casually announcing that I had led Sara to Christ. I threw it out there like it was an everyday occurrence. It seemed so natural to me; my parents were the ones flabbergasted. I calmly explained that Sara didn't know Jesus, and I wanted to make sure she understood how much He loved her, and I wanted to see her again in heaven, so she prayed and asked Jesus into her heart.

MISSING

As an adult I look back at the child me and I laugh. I'm also a little appalled. Who was I to be evangelizing the playground? But isn't that just the point? Who better to reach kids but kids? I went where no adult would go and struck up a conversation about my friend Jesus with my new friend Sara. What resulted was, I believe, a God-ordained moment on the jungle gym.

We must not underestimate how God can and is going to use kids in the lives of other kids. I have story after story of kids who have led their friends to Jesus. Nothing brings me more joy than a kid telling me that the friend they've been praying for has started a relationship with Jesus. I love it! They may have started the ball rolling by bringing their friend to church, but they're the ones who are day in, day out, in their lives.

Chong Wang. I'll never forget that name or his cute little face. From a stout Chinese Buddhist family, Chong was allowed to come to our midweek youth group for fourth through sixth graders because his friend Ben had invited him. Chong was in fifth grade, spoke English as a second language, and had a smile that wouldn't quit. He made me laugh every single week.

We went deep in our group and Chong went somewhat warily with us. He had been Buddhist his whole life, so this whole Jesus thing was new to him. Our adult team loved on him and the kids treated him like anyone else. Ben was extremely burdened for Chong and prayed faithfully for him. My team and I joined Ben in praying for him. I talked to Chong when he had questions and pointed him to Jesus. And then it happened, the day Ben came to me to tell me, "Miss Mel, Chong asked Jesus into his heart last night!" He was beaming and a little teary. I hugged him and was a lot teary. Chong had kept asking questions and Ben kept answering and finally Chong was ready. Ben was able to pray with him.

It was a beautiful moment and a beautiful lesson to me. I was not rejoicing any less because Ben had led Chong to the Lord instead of me. In fact, I was delighted that Ben had been able to be a part of Chong's decision. He had prayed faithfully and fervently, and God had answered his prayers. It was a life-changing moment for both of them.

The next time I saw Chong, he smiled a little brighter. I went up to him and told him how excited I was that he had started a relationship with Jesus. He ducked his head and kept smiling.

As time went on, Ben and I made sure he had a Bible, and Chong stayed involved in our group and eventually moved on to youth group. I moved away and stayed remotely in touch with him via Facebook.

In 2013 as a junior in high school, Chong died in his sleep, a victim of Young Asian Death Syndrome. In a moment his heart stopped beating and his life on earth ended. While I mourn his death, I find great joy in knowing that he is sitting with Jesus, all because of a child. One child passionate about Jesus changed the course of another child's life. Don't underestimate the impact of a child.

Don't underestimate a child's ability to understand God.

I think we as adults tend to overcomplicate God. I had a period in ministry where I was reluctant to extend an invitation for kids to accept Jesus because I couldn't figure out how to explain the atoning sacrifice to them and the importance of covenant. Good grief! I laugh about that now, but at the time I was seriously conflicted. I didn't want to make it too hard for them. In my desire to not make it too hard, I made it ridiculously complicated.

Kids are straightforward, they're literal, and they're honest. Most of them also have a gift of faith that rivals any adults. As complicated as we want to make it, Jesus is really quite simple. Keep it simple and allow God to do the work. Step back in amazement at what He does and what kids understand.

Recently I had a conversation with a six-year-old girl about the Trinity. The minute she brought it up, sweat broke out on my forehead. There is probably nothing I find harder to explain to kids than the Trinity. And here was this adorable girl asking me how God and Jesus and the Holy Spirit were all the same.

I'm not proud to admit that I, a national children's disciple-making specialist and a children's ministry innovator, was failing miserable in my explanation. The six year old was listening intently as I stumbled my way through. I can't remember the last time I stuttered like that. I rambled on and on until she stopped me, "Oh I get it Miss Mel!"

"You do?" Of course I was thinking, "I'm not sure I even get it anymore, isn't there a teacher around?"

She grabbed a handful of her hair, "So like the hair on my head is hair, but it's also just hair?"

"Okay."

Then she tugged one of her eyebrows between two little fingers, "And my eyebrows are my eyebrows, but they're also hair."

"Keep going."

Lastly, she pinched her eyelashes and squinted at me, "And my eyelashes are eyelashes, but they're also hair. Is that what you mean?"

I sat there for what felt like two full minutes, but was probably more like 10 seconds, with my mouth hanging open.

"Yes! Yes, that's exactly what I mean. You're amazing!" She giggled as I gave her a big hug.

I had just been schooled by a six-year-old girl wearing a yellow sundress. That was the best explanation for the Trinity I had ever heard. It was so good I blogged it and then pinned it on Pinterest with the title "hairy Trinity."

I had vastly underestimated her ability to understand the trinity because I had put her in a box of my own inabilities. God is at work in kids; we cannot underestimate what He can and will do in and through them.

Last but not least, don't underestimate their stories. I've touched on this throughout, so I'm not going to belabor this point. Do not assume that you understand the world in which they are living. Go back and read through the statistics, reread the stories, or better yet talk to kids you know. We have no idea what they're going through and what their world looks like.

Every single time I think I have figured out kids and their stories, I am put back in my place. I am trying so hard to learn what I'm writing here, to not underestimate the depth and breadth of their stories.

One of my trademarks as a camp speaker is that I ask the staff to share their stories. When I'm new to a camp, I inevitably get pushback when I ask for volunteers to share their testimonies. Their excuses run the gamut, and their hearts are truly in the right place. They don't feel like their stories of depression, suicidal thoughts, bullying, abuse, neglect, fear, anger, and more should be told to kids. They're wrong and they're always surprised when I tell them that.

One of the main reasons I allow other people to tell their stories is that I only have my story and it won't connect with every kid. When I allow other stories to be told, more kids are able to connect. Also, it's so good for the staff (usually college students) to practice openness and vulnerability with kids. It's also so good (and hard) for me and the staff to hear the kids' stories as they respond.

A young man who talked about bullying had both boys and girls talking to him all week and sharing their stories of bullying and thanking him for sharing. A young woman who shared about growing up in a foster home had an extremely unique connection with one little girl who was living the same story. She was able to minister to her in a way I never could have. The staff member who shared about struggling with depression had a number of kids come and talk to her and me. We met kids as young as second grade who were taking depression medicine.

After hearing a story of abuse, a little guy who had been a ray of sunshine all week at camp asked to talk to me. He and his sister sat down across from me and told me their story of neglect and abuse and their ultimate adoption into a new family. "I was found in a closet with a broken leg when I was three." I had assumed he had grown up in the large loving family that he was a part of. I had assumed he had always been safe and well cared for. I had underestimated his story.

After hearing a staff member share about adoption, a young Ecuadorian girl asked if she could share her story. Adopted at age 10, she told me she never thought a life like this could be possible. She was used to living on the street and had expected that to be her life. In her newly learned English she said, "Now I have family, now I know Jesus, now I am safe, and now I am scared no more." I had assumed she was adopted as a baby and had experienced a fairly typical life. I had underestimated her story.

Kids need adults who don't underestimate them. They need adults who pass on faith and believe they can change the world and point others to Jesus. They need adults who understand they have a huge capacity to understand and love Jesus. They need adults who refuse to assume they understand and who are willing to listen to their stories. They need us to step it up and stop underestimating them.

The call is before you, what you do with it is up to you. My prayer is that you will join with me in rescuing this generation of kids. My prayer is that you as the church will have new eyes to see what is before you. Most of all, my prayer is that you will continually and consistently depend on our never missing, never late, never frantic, and never changing God. This 4/14 Window will only be reached by us first yielding ourselves to Him. The call is there, what will you do?

BONUS CHAPTER FOR LEADERS

LEADERS

If you currently serve as a children's ministry leader, this little section is for you. I may unpack these things in another book, but for right now these are some things I'm saying over and over again to leaders everywhere I go.

CURRICULUM

Don't reinvent the wheel. There is great curriculum out there! Don't stress yourself out with trying to write your own curriculum. Instead, adapt what there is to fit you.

Curriculum doesn't run you or your program—you run your curriculum. Don't depend on it to make you who you are. Find out who you are as a church body and make it work for you.

Don't assume it's a curriculum problem. Ninety-five percent of the time a curriculum issue is brought to me, it's not an actual curriculum problem, it's a leadership issue. Are you equipping your volunteers to use the curriculum? Are you casting vision? Are you showing them how it works? Evaluate yourself.

STOP

The number one thing I say when I consult in churches is "stop." When did it become normal and okay for the church to be everything to all people? Take a break and reevaluate:

Why are you doing what you're doing?

What purpose is it accomplishing? Is it needed?

Is it effective?

Is it sustainable?

Are you overworking your volunteers/staff?

If you don't have an answer for ALL of those questions, then take a step back. You do not have to do it all. Instead of running in circles doing a lot of stuff, stop for a minute and do the right things on purpose. That may mean not doing VBS, a mid-week program, mommy and me, craft night, etc. And guess what, that's okay.

Find your niche. Just like we all have a place in the body of Christ, I firmly believe each church body has a place where they fit best. Stop trying to be like the church down the street, and figure out who you are. Do some soul searching with your leadership team and find where you fit. What can you do that another church can't? Where do you naturally have inroads? Start there and work your way out. Allow God to show you his plan and heart for your ministry and church body instead of doing things and then asking them to be God's plans. Stop.

SHEPHERD

Whether your title has the word pastor in it or not, if you are in leadership in a church, you are called to be a shepherd. (On a side note, if you have a relationship with Jesus, you're in ministry.) Don't underestimate yourself and don't underestimate your influence. It's easy to take on the role of shepherd to kids, it's not as easy to realize you need to also be shepherding your volunteers. Your volunteers are a gift to you and you must shepherd them with care. Stop seeing them as people who fill holes in your schedule and start seeing them as people who need shepherding. Care more about their souls and their well-being than you do about the blanks on your schedule. If you're recruiting the kind of people we talked about in the section regarding adults, then you have quality people. Treat them as such and shepherd them.

Check in with them. Find out how they're really doing.

Observe them. Are they filled with joy? Are they prepared? Are they excited?

Give them breaks. Don't ever expect someone to serve indefinitely.

Make sure they are getting time in "big church."

Pray for them by name. Do it.

Thank them regularly. Notes, gifts, verbal praise. Be intentional.

Have the hard conversations with them. If their marriage is in trouble, or their soul is weary, be up front with them. Speak words of life over them and release them from ministry for awhile.

Deal with the hard stuff. You deal with the kid who won't stop biting the doorframe or the helper volunteer who is always texting. Let them have a win every Sunday; you take on the hard stuff.

Equip them. Give them tools. Train them. Come alongside them and then ...

Release them. Allow them to flourish without you hovering or micromanaging. Train them and let them fly.

IT'S HIS MINISTRY, NOT YOURS

It's not your ministry; it's God's. And guess what? He's never surprised when you're short a teacher, never shocked that little Henry threw up, never panicked over your student to teacher ratio, and he never lies in bed at night worrying over the VBS schedule. He is, and was, and always has been. He's in control and He's perfect. He's called you and equipped you, but He hasn't left you on your own. It's His ministry, not yours. Don't ever hold it so tightly you allow yourself to fall into the trap of arrogance or pride or allow yourself to believe your self-worth is tied up in what you do. It's His. Release it, surrender, and be filled with great joy and peace.

SOUL CARE

My heart's cry for you, leader, is that you would find your sense of worth, your belonging, and your identity in Jesus and Jesus alone. Ministry is hard. There is no denying it. The rosy glow only lasts for a minute, and then suddenly you realize that people are sinners and Christians are some of the worst. Your soul can be sucked dry. However, if you expect to lead well, you must first take care of your soul. Stop running yourself ragged and take care of you. Find what feeds your soul and make it a regular part of your schedule. Go for long walks, sing worship music at the top of your lungs, take a three-day retreat a few times each year, go shopping by yourself, have coffee with a good friend, go to the gym. Whatever it is, do it. Spend time with Jesus as often as you can, tune your ear to His voice, and put yourself back in the role you were created to be in, to be loved and cared for by your Creator. If you find yourself believing you are the savior of your ministry or that "one" kid, then I guarantee you your soul needs some attention. Never apologize for soul care, and always make it a priority. Out of the abundance of what you receive, may you pour into others and pass on faith.

ABOUT THE AUTHOR

The daughter of a pastor and the oldest sister of three, Melissa grew up doing ministry with her family. Melissa herself has been a children's pastor and missionary. Passionate about the church and about kids, she travels extensively speaking, training, coaching, and consulting. She currently serves as the national Children's Disciplemaking Specialist for the Christian and Missionary Alliance denomination. She's been to over 30 countries and seeks out the best ethnic food in every city she visits.

melissajmacdonald.com
Twitter: @kidsconsultant
Facebook: /kidsconsultant